1000
Dessous

1000 Dessous

A History of Lingerie
Eine Geschichte der Reizwäsche
Histoire de la Lingerie

Gilles Néret

TASCHEN

KÖLN LISBOA LONDON NEW YORK PARIS TOKYO

Contents

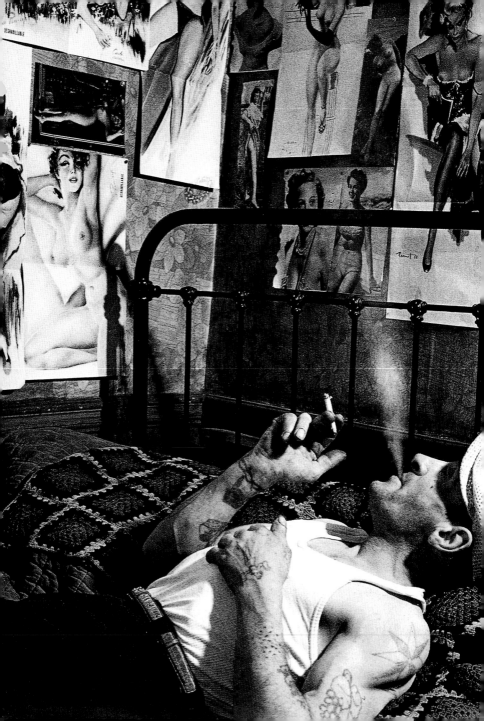

The Venus Fly-trap

Women's lingerie is the stuff of fantasy. A vital element in the skilled art of undressing, it never fails to work its strange magic on the male libido. The sex is prosaic unless seen through a veil that emphasises its forbidden attractions. In the words of Montaigne: "There are things best displayed by concealment."

Women have worn underwear since the dawn of civilisation, sometimes openly, sometimes secretly, as the social climate dictated. Society frequently advanced hypocritical pretexts for the wearing of lingerie, invoking dubious reasons of health and hygiene. No-one was willing to admit the truth, that these clinging undergarments, these "snares of Venus" clothed the erotic life of eras perverse, brutal or lascivious. In so doing, they sated the fantasies of the women who placed these diabolical contrivances upon their bodies, and the men who delighted in taking them off again. *Ribbons, petticoats, corsets, drawers, brassieres* and *knickers* have all played their part in the mysterious *pas de deux* by which man and woman have been united since time immemorial.

The "magnificent slut" and the fetichist

According to Hirschfeld, of 1,000 men surveyed only 350 were attracted to wholly naked women; 400 men preferred them half-dressed, and 250 showed a marked preference for fully-clothed women. In other words, 65% of men showed fetishist tendencies. This is the voice of Faust, crying out in an ecstasy of love: "Bring me a fichu that has covered her breast, a ribbon that belongs to my love!"

The history of lingerie, from its origins to the height of its glory in film and advertising, is an epic one. Its burden is this: women have always treated the need to cover up and the desire to uncover as a pretext for enhancing their feminine allure. So take your seats, ladies and gentlemen, the show is about to begin: the curtain rises like a skirt to reveal an indecorous *décor* of lingerie. Sit back and enjoy the performance; it may continue later behind closed doors.

The earliest undergarments for women date back to 2,000 BC in Crete: the *crinoline* and the *corset*. But Cretan women, whom Elie Faure describes as "dolls" and Jacques Laurent as "magnificent sluts", merely wore these figure-hugging garments to lift and accentuate their bare breasts or to emphasise their hips, making their bodies seem

◀ Pin-ups are the stuff of dreams. Photograph by Robert Doisneau. Circa 1950 more voluptuous. Women in ancient Greece wore a *zona* under their gown. This was a type of girdle, a band of cloth or leather, whose only purpose was to accentuate the figure and emphasise femininity. Similarly, Roman women wore tight-fitting, jewelled *garters* around their thighs. These garters were not there to hold up *stockings,* which had not yet been invented; their sole purpose was to arouse men's fetishist desires. For Roman men, the girdles, scarves and embroidered fabrics that had enwrapped the most treasurable parts of a woman's body possessed an erotic charge, just as they had done for the Greeks. The birth of a fetishist cult, which was to continue through the ages, is evidenced by the popular saying *"zonam solvere"*, which means literally "to untie the girdle" and, by extension, "to marry". The *cestus,* an embroidered corset sheathing the body from the groin to the base of the breast was, as the myth goes, designed by none other than Venus, who strongly recommended it to Juno, a goddess endowed with an overly voluptuous figure. Martial described it as a snare from which no man could escape, a device admirably suited to the rekindling of the flames of love; he himself was aroused by the thought of touching a *cestus* "still warm from Venus's fire".

The utopian garters of Thélème and the pageboy thighs of the Renaissance

Women's realisation that one way of arousing passion in men was to give free rein to their own passion for underwear and thus accentuate the natural differences between the sexes is not, then, a recent one. Woman selected their lingerie to serve as a continual reminder to their lovers that women were indeed a breed apart. Lingerie was no less popular in the Middle Ages. Women did not wear knickers, which were thought to prevent them airing their private parts and warming them at the hearth. Instead, the *gipon* was invented. Far from emphasising the breasts, this new type of corset was worn to flatten them, placing greater emphasis on the stomach, which was regarded as a monument to femininity. For this reason, women also wore padding to enhance the overall effect. The Middle Ages was a golden age for lingerie: it was during this period that undergarments became a vehicle for fetishism and the garter became a particularly erotic accessory. In his novel *Gargantua,* Rabelais described the dress of the licentious ladies of the Abbey of Thélème, who liked to wear garters that matched their bracelets.

In the Renaissance, Italian art was transformed by the work of such renowned homosexual artists as Leonardo da Vinci, Botticelli, Michelangelo and Raphael.

Applying brush and chisel, they created a variety of ambiguous creatures: male torsos sprouting female breasts, chaste madonnas with the hot eyes of beautiful young men. Lingerie swiftly followed suit with the invention of the *vertugade* or French farthingale. This was a hooped petticoat, comprising wooden bands, thick wire and padded rolls; it was worn to make the female body look more masculine by eliminating the prominent stomach so popular in the Middle Ages. In other words, it was an obvious attempt to bring underwear into line with the homosexual aesthetic. Maria de' Medici, an avid supporter of sexual equality, was said to have started the subsequent fashion for wearing *pantaloons,* also known as drawers or, more eloquently, *brides à fesses* ("bottom-huggers"), which demonstrated women's desire to show off their legs like men. Brantôme notes that these pantaloons were open at the crotch, enabling women to give themselves to their lovers without disrobing, a practical consideration when consorting in corridors. Pantaloons protected women against dust and cold, he observes, but regrets that they concealed legs and other parts from sight when their wearers tumbled off a horse or slipped. He added: "Pantaloons also protect women from dissolute young men; a hand slipped under a petticoat cannot meet with bare flesh." However, it soon became obvious that the wearing of pantaloons made of cloth of gold or braided and embroidered fabric adorned with precious stones had more to do with exhibitionism than modesty. At a time when homosexuality was widespread, pantaloons, far from being chaste, merely allowed women to present their thighs like page boys.

"The modest", "the wanton" and the birdcage

During the Reformation, preachers described farthingales and drawers as "diabolical contrivances". A return to wholesome femininity, indeed, wholesome nudity, resulted, which sealed the fate of drawers. In the 17th century, they were replaced by the petticoat. This loose-fitting undergarment allowed air to circulate freely. It was composed of three layers, named according to their strategic position: "le modeste", "le fripon" (the wanton) and finally "le secret". The names given to lingerie were now more honest, reflecting its guilty intentions. The décolleté bodice was called "la gourgandine" (the hussy). Montaigne described the corset as "a type of girdle encasing the bust from the base of the breast to below the ribcage, ending in a point over the stomach". In France, its more daring variants gave rise to suggestive and colourful names: "le mousquetaire" (the musketeer), "l'innocente" (the innocent), "la culbute" (the tumble), "les guêpes" (the wasps), "le boute-en-train" (the live-wire), "le tâtez-y" (the come-on), "les engageantes" (the flirts), "l'effrontée" (the brazen hussy), "la criarde" (the show-off), etc.. The first advertising slogan appeared in a corset-maker's window, promoting a style that could, it boasted, "control the strong, support the weak, and return the errant to the straight and narrow!" As Jacques Laurent points out: "Throughout the ages, women have felt the need to squeeze, strangle and compress hips and breasts and, from the bands worn by Athenian women to the girdles worn today, not excluding the corset of recent memory, have invariably contrived to satisfy this need."

The 18th century saw the invention of the *pannier,* a type of birdcage (oh for the plumes of that bird!). Suspended from the waist, it was made of wicker hoops, tapes and whalebone. It immediately came under fire from the moralists, who considered it the ultimate in provocation. One of these moralists, Father Bridaine, accused fashionable ladies of wanting "to live and die in a state of impenitence, weighed down forever by the great weight of their scandalous, burdensome panniers". He credited "this seductive lure" with the power to "incite poor, unhappy men to sin". For the pannier did not merely emphasise the buttocks. By opening a gap between body and gown, it also made them more alluring and accessible. As there is no stopping the march of progress, the pannier was soon replaced by a simple *bustle,* known more explicitly in French as a *faux cul* (literally, "false bum"). This was supposed to allow the woman greater freedom of movement but in fact focused attention on her backside. French women were consequently to be heard uttering remarks which could easily be misinterpreted, and were borrowed by writers seeking to spice up their more frivolous productions: "Good morning, my dear, let me see your bum… But, my dear, your bum is simply terrible! It's narrow, niggardly and it droops; it's awful! If you want to see a nice one, take a look at mine."

Napoleon's corset, the voyeur's crinoline and Zola's split drawers

Between two campaigns, Napoleon took the time to express his views on the corset, writing to his physician, Corvisart: "This garment, tasteless in its coquetry, this garment that tortures women and harms their unborn children, warns of frivolous tastes and makes me fear imminent decadence." The "frivolous tastes" were not long in coming. By the end of the Empire, the prevailing fashion was for well-separated breasts, a look achieved by wearing a whalebone contraption devised by the corset-maker, Leroy. Solutions are found to the most exacting dictates of fashion.

At the turn of the 19th century, when long drawers threatened to reappear under the name of pantaloons, the French government was at pains to reassure women that they would not be obliged to wear them. An open and loose-fitting style of dress was not against "Republican morals". In fact, the fashion industry eagerly appropriated pantaloons, making them more feminine. They were now transparent, richly embroidered and were so long that they showed below the dress, again catching the eye. These little adjustments sufficed; pantaloons came back with a vengeance, winning that ultimate accolade, the approval of courtesans.

In 1840, when hemlines came down again, the *crinoline,* that much-improved descendant of the pannier and the French farthingale, provided redress. By holding the woman's clothes away from her body, it made it possible to catch a glimpse of what lay beneath. The sight of a woman in a crinoline gliding downstairs, leaning back to steady her balance, was much appreciated by connoisseurs. Just as when a woman emerges from a car today, much was revealed. And the lingerie-makers did not rest on their laurels. For women of easy virtue, they created little drawers that were "virtually see-through and so amusing, with that long, long opening which seems to go on forever". In Emile Zola's novel *L'Assommoir,* when Virginie is spanked in the wash house, she sports drawers with an open crotch, as does Nana in the novel by Zola of the same name. Both novels have been filmed.

Freud and the many-layered woman

After the fat years come the lean years. This loose-fitting style of dress was soon replaced by an extremely restrictive fashion. By 1900, women's clothes were more restrictive than ever. Not only did dresses resemble straitjackets, but a profusion of undergarments protected women against the remotest chance of assault. In fact, it was difficult for a well-bred adolescent in France's Belle Epoque to form any notion of the shape of a woman. Their clothed bodies presented a peculiar appearance: a massive corset, a veritable instrument of torture worthy of the sadomasochist repertory, stretched from their shoulders to their thighs. In addition, they also wore a long chemise, an under-bodice, several petticoats and a pair of knickers. Peeling this onion might indeed reduce one to tears.

These constrictions were soon undone. Women's bodies were all but armour-plated? Very well, this was grist to the mill of dear old Freud, who was researching into the libido of his contemporaries. In particular, he was eliciting their attitudes to underwear, which was now, for the first time, used to frustrate amorous advances, and thus proffered the taboo as an incitement to debauch. The woman's suit of armour soon exploded. The strip-tease was born, making a performance of the slow and involved act of undressing; the Americans soon become past masters of the art. In Paris, Toulouse-Lautrec, an enthusiast, went to see many performances of the "Coucher d'Yvette" (Yvette's Bedtime Routine) with his friends. The first girlie magazines were also invented. One such was *La Vie Parisienne,* a forerunner of *Playboy,* which enabled men to examine every item of women's lingerie (almost) as closely as they desired. This was the heyday of the music-hall in Montmartre, when girls in black stockings and frothy underwear gave bourgeois men a chance to cast off their inhibitions in public.

Woman as furniture, fetters as fashion

The layers enveloping women in the 1900s matched the Art Nouveau style then in vogue. As Jacques Laurent remarks, corsets reflect prevailing design trends: "In general, women and furniture evolve on the same lines. The resemblance between a French Directory chair and a woman wearing a tunic is like that between the S-shaped woman of the 1900s and the S-shapes of table legs, brooches and Art Nouveau entrances to the Paris Metro. It is as if, around 1890, fashions mutated, and this change was reflected in the female body as in the Gallé coffee table."

With every burst of artillery fire during the 1914-1918 war, skirts rose by two centimetres, revealing first the calf, then the knee. The fast-shrinking corset was soon reduced to a mere suspender belt, worn around the waist and next to the skin. Fashionable ladies gradually came to prefer this to garters, which restricted the circulation of blood. Women relaxed, revelling in their new-found freedom: they went horse-riding, played tennis and took holidays by the sea. Dumping ballast like a hot-air balloon, fashion became lighter and lighter. The modern brassiere was invented and thick stockings were re-placed by silk. Until 1930, eroticism took up residence in that magical place between stocking-top and knickers, in the strip of bare skin glimpsed when a woman crossed her legs or got out of a car. "That fold of flesh," comments Jacques Laurent, "calls to mind a bracelet , if not indeed a shackle. And it signals a region of the body defenceless to the waist, or better still, all the way to the breast, given that dresses and slips are rarely close-fitting."

"Petit Bateau", parachute and suspender belt

Next on the scene were the sensible French "Petit Bateau" knickers. These were pure white, made of ribbed cotton, and might be seen if the wind were right. For Japanese men, they were a cult object, especially when worn by schoolgirls in uniform. Women's lingerie had now been scaled down to the "bare" minimum: bra, knickers and suspender belt. But women who wore little or nothing beneath their dresses held little or no appeal for fetishists, or indeed for manufacturers. It was a temporary setback. As always, when fashion lacks imagination, designers take their inspiration from the past. In this case, it was nostalgic memories of the black lacy underwear worn by women of the night, and the frilly knickers of French cancan dancers. This marked the return of the "Coucher d'Yvette" and Victorian underwear. The erotic spotlight returned to the leg, which was often to be found waving in the air in the course of the fashionable charleston. Suspender belts became more discreet and were worn primarily to be removed. At the same time, a new figure captivated men's minds: the vamp. Out went passive women who would capitulate after two fainting fits and three ritual refusals, and the *femme fatale*, the "Blue Angel", became the new sex symbol.

Alas, women barely had time to enjoy peacetime and rediscover, along with their bodies, their new-found power over men — at dances, for example, when their partners found it difficult to hide their arousal at teasing glimpses of bare thigh glimpsed above silk stockings; the world was again plunged into war. For the sensualist too, these were the years of blackout. The lingerie industry could not obtain new materials for its products and parachutes took priority over suspender belts. In the cities, women eked out their pre-war lingerie or simulated the appearance of stockings with dye; the finishing touch was a fake seam drawn up the back of the leg with a crayon.

Soldiers, however, continued to indulge their fantasies. The vamp was followed by the pin-up, who had just become popular in the U.S.A. GIs would cut their picture out of magazines and pin them up on the barracks wall, above their bed, hence the name. They would be fixed to the radiator of a truck or stuck onto the fuselage of an aeroplane, which is why Ava Gardner was suspected of dropping the atom bomb on

Hiroshima. The GIs fighting in the Pacific were desperate for new heroines to beguile the monotony of evenings confined to camp. Rita Hayworth's black satin underwear knocked them for six. Jean Harlow's explosively beautiful rival was outright winner in the contest to occupy the GI's solitary daydreams. In 1940, Hayworth was the sex symbol *par excellence*. In the film *Gilda,* she strips off a long-sleeved glove with the gestures of a woman removing her stocking or knickers.

Breasts like artillery shells and the barbed bra

Since then, pin-up girls have taken the world by storm. They have invaded the tabloid press, advertisements, calendars and playing cards. They are presented in ingenious states of undress by illustrators and photographers who have no other aim than that of arousing men. All in the best English manner, of course; look, but don't touch. Their one purpose is to seduce men. With laudable zeal, they model themselves on the original sex symbols, film stars like Betty Grable, Rita Hayworth, Ava Gardner, Jayne Mansfield, Marilyn Monroe and Brigitte Bardot, to name but a few. They are, let us confess, a bit vulgar: all cosmetic colours, pert breasts and buttocks, they display the sleek curves of a Cadillac. They are clearly brand new and squeaky-clean as only American women can be as they disport themselves in their uniform of transparent garments and lingerie. The curve of their backs takes your breath away, their breasts are like artillery shells, their buttocks are flawless, their legs extend into the distance like motorways, and their bellies are as flat and smooth as a beach at low tide. In other words, they are essentially a collage of clichés, with a single aim: the popular sanctification of sex. The setting counts for nothing. No creativity is lavished on the pin-up. But the flesh dazzles in its specialised packaging of flimsy nudity.

Pin-ups are used to sell all types of products. In days gone by, their ancestors, the good-time girls, used to promote a brand of cocoa or oil. Pin-up girls in a consumer society take part in events organised by deodorant or dishwasher companies. This is a far remove indeed from the amoral, carefree *grisette* of the turn of the century, always spread out on capacious divans or sprawled in the bathtub, concerned only with her plumes, poses and lovers, and priding herself on her haughty reserve. Modern-day pin-ups, on the contrary, are shameless: they are kitted out with boots, whips, pointy bras and leather or vinyl suspender belts with dildos attached. Eager to inflict torture or be tortured, they open their brazen legs. They have become the symbols of our age of warrior sexuality.

Dior's New Look and Fellini's strip-tease

The end of the Second World War ushered in a new era of prosperity and Christian Dior's revolutionary New Look, in 1947, made up for a lengthy period of forced abstinence in terms of luxury products, leading to a soaring demand for lingerie. The breast was no longer in hiding as it had been in the war, but nestled loosely in silk like a dove. Sexual archetypes dating back to classical antiquity came back into vogue: tiny waist, rounded hips and large breasts. Howard Hughes designed the half-cup bra between two fuselages and with it launched his latest protégée, Jane Russell, into the Hollywood firmament. By now, fashions in lingerie could be dictated by the silver screen.

In the voyeur's darkroom, the magic lantern stealthily filled spectators' hearts with its fantasies. Ever since the birth of cinema, extremely powerful moral factions in the United States, like the Catholic Legion of Decency, had endeavoured to clip its wings. But they had not bargained on the inventiveness of film-makers, who quickly realised that scanty underwear was far more suggestive than the nude and devoted their talents to portraying every possible variation on this tantalising theme.

From that time onwards, every film star has taken part in this secret battle against censorship, appearing resplendent and subversive in knickers or suspender belts. On screen, a state of undress can be a filmset in its own right and the act of undressing an end in itself. Fellini's striptease scene (Nadia Gray in *La Dolce Vita*) is as memorable as Vittorio de Sica's (Sophia Loren in *Yesterday, Today and Tomorrow*). The "vamp" (half-closed eyes, heavy make-up, pouting lips, cigarette, provocative pose, prominent breasts), in sexy black underwear, is a sister in perversity to the "ingénue" in white underwear (wide eyes, no apparent make-up, mouth open to reveal dazzling white teeth, modest bearing, small breasts).

The blackstocking Blue Angel and the Cardinal's Baby Doll

The common confusion between "appât", the French word for "lure", (dictionary definition: bait used to attract prey, fish… Anything which attracts, incites someone to do something) and "appas", the French word used to describe an attractive woman's appearance (figuratively: charms, appeal…) is a revealing one. In film, the two meanings merge into one. One embodiment of the tension between the censor's constraints and the film-maker's ingenuity is the femme fatale, Lola-Lola, in *The Blue Angel* by Josef von

Sternberg. The puritanical Professor Unrath, played by Emil Jannings, is a mere mortal and cannot resist the temptations of Marlene Dietrich, the epitome of vampish womanhood, sexily dressed in a bristling period suspender belt, her legs "sheathed in their own venom" (Audiberti). This marked another crushing defeat for the moralists. Happily, it was not the last. The surrender of the respectable pillar of society to the voluptuous and implacable she-devil in sexy underwear proved a successful formula. In its wake came Bob Fosse's *Cabaret*, Fassbinder's *Marriage of Maria Braun* and its sequel, *Lola,* not to mention films by Edward Dmytryk and many others. Emulators of Marlene Dietrich, such as Liza Minnelli, Barbara Sukowa, Hanna Schygulla, May Britt and Hildegard Knef handed down Dietrich's invaluable props: suspender belt and black stockings.

The more virulent the condemnation, the more useful it proves. Purple-faced, Cardinal Spellman launched into an apoplectic diatribe that shook the very recent Gothic vaults of St Patrick's Cathedral. "Whoever dares to see this film, whoever dares look upon this shameless woman, is committing a mortal sin. Never in this god-fearing country has anything so revolting, disgusting, indeed so scurrilous, been placed before our eyes." This blistering denunciation referred not to *The Blue Angel* but to another cult film, *Baby Doll,* made in 1956 by Elia Kazan. Kazan's mortal sin was to show Carroll Baker in a babydoll nightie, sucking her thumb. The Cardinal's rage did more to promote the film than all the advertising agencies put together. By citing her digital fellatio, Spellman helped raise the admirers of that act to 65% in the subsequent *Kinsey Report.* And finally, his fulmination had the not inconsiderable effect of boosting sales of "babydoll" nighties to the tune of 25 million. Thanks to the Church's intervention, the film industry was able to promote sales of lingerie.

Paper dames for schoolboys and phaenomerides in tights

Christian Dior's post-war New Look, as we have seen, brought back the corset, with its accompanying throng of erotic memories. The new smaller style of corset was called a "waspie" or bustier, depending on whether it was designed to clinch the waist or support the breasts. Men were more than happy with this retro fashion. The schoolboys of the 1950s were also catered for. A French magazine, no longer in existence, called *Paris-Hollywood* took care of their education. They would flick through it feverishly in secret, discovering women who looked nothing like their mothers. This magazine showed its girls in varying stages of undress, performing an expert striptease for the delectation of its solitary readers. Luxuriant blonde hair cascaded over their well-turned shoulders and strips of lace stretched over their thighs to hold up the inevitable black stockings. (At this time, black stockings were worn by ladies of the night, unless the ladies were black themselves and wore white.) These pin-ups never took off the stiletto shoes in which their feet arched to breathtaking effect. One-dimensional women in ritual and bewitching dress, they struck poses designed to arouse the magazine's reader-voyeurs. In the U.S.A, their equivalents wore still more vertiginous stilettos.

Although lingerie seemed to have come into its own in this favourable climate, storm clouds were gathering. On a black day for fetishists, in the 1960s, Mary Quant, a former model, launched the miniskirt. Thighs exposed spelled disaster for suspender belts, which had no option but to beat a hasty retreat. The inevitable consequence of the miniskirt was the invention of tights or pantyhose. This one-piece, known in France by the brand name *Mitoufle*, combined stockings and knickers. But its longer counterpart, the body stocking, could encase a woman from feet to shoulders, like a potato in its jacket. Freedom had been short-lived indeed. The miniskirt marked a return to the straitjacket. Feminist movements hung out the flags: down with "women as sex objects", long live "sexless women". Advertisements echoed these sentiments, proclaiming: "Suspenders go out of fashion!" Young women were exhorted to wear the panty girdle, which boasted orthopaedic qualities. This practical undergarment was a pair of knickers and corset all in one, and what was more, it could "flatten your stomach and help you shed 6lb at one go".

But lingerie cannot survive without its old accomplice, eroticism. A counter-attack was in the making. Not that there was anything aesthetically wrong with this new fashion. On the contrary, the Athenians had long ago dubbed young Spartan women "phaenomerides" or "women-who-show-their-thighs". The banished stocking could make a comeback in the form of hold-ups (stockings that stay up on their own). These were well suited to being worn with miniskirts; they came up very high and were sheerer than tights. Tights themselves, under permanent threat from the dictates of fashion and the demands of male libido, were adorned with seams in imitation of stockings, in a bid to acquire a sexier image. Advertising ceased to boast of their irrelevant practical qualities and attempted to impart an element of fantasy to this most prosaic of garments.

Marilyn's knickers, Madonna's suspender belts

Once again, girlie magazines like *Playboy* and *Penthouse* came to the rescue. They exhibited their usual assortment of women in seductive outfits. The film industry too entered the fray, never missing an opportunity to reveal Marilyn Monroe's knickers or Sophia Loren's suspender belt. When lingerie is imperilled, the best remedy is a dose of retro. The suspender had seemed extinct; now it made a timid reappearance. But its significance had completely changed. When worn by Madonna, it acquired the force of a manifesto. It was no longer a symbol of slavery, as people had maintained. Now it announced the liberation of the dominatrix. It had graduated from practical accessory to vehicle of the emotions. This development was not lost on Jacques Laurent, high priest of lingerie and member of the *Académie française*. "A woman used to wear a suspender belt under her skirt innocently and as a matter of course, whereas she now knows that this deliberate act has a significance for her and for others," he noted. But this significance had become subtler. Freed of its function, the suspender belt reached new heights of significance. It now operates as a special bond between the woman who wears it and the man who has access to it. In the past, it was worn out of necessity, now it is worn for pleasure. And, first and foremost, for the narcissistic pleasure of gazing at a beautiful reflection in the mirror and revelling in the sensual touch of delicate nylon against bare skin; in other words, of feeling good, of feeling ultra-feminine. Then comes a second consideration: the desire to establish a hierarchy between women who do and women who do not wear them. The hierarchy becomes apparent when a woman wearing one publicly crosses her legs or rearranges her skirt in such a way as to show that she is different, thereby angering her rivals who are not wearing one and consider it an unfair advantage. At the risk of humiliating the male sex, we must report that only in third place comes the secret code that regulates women's relationships with men: "Look, I am revealing a little, I am revealing a little more!" Suspender belts have thus lost their innocence and become a coded language, the password for entry into an exclusive club. Some women wear them only for those occasions when their expectations are high. Some put them on to go to bed. In a word, some of us believe that suspender belts are the prerogative of a superior kind of woman, bold enough to exploit all her assets, the "feminine woman", a new concept which has made the notion of the "woman as sex object" obsolete. Others still support the idea of desexualisation and dream of rivalling men in a domain that is essentially feminine. Such women bitterly deride all male fetishism, and are particularly hostile towards those of their sisters who deck themselves out to indulge neurotic male fantasies. On the other hand, the sinners themselves know that, in the words of Empress Catherine II, "the temptress soon becomes the tempted".

The admen and the slave of industry

These circumstances do not facilitate the task of the admen. A new and subtle technique is required in the matter of lingerie, one that runs counter to the adman's usual approach. Magazines losing market share wonder "Does sex still sell?" and then show that it does by using sex to increase their circulation. By contrast, the advertising industry has realised that underwear and sex are not necessarily a good fit. Sex can be used to sell most things, particularly to men. But underwear belongs to an essentially feminine world in which the woman has become a product in her own right, "an industrial slave", as Klossowski puts it: star, model, hostess, bourgeoise, peasant, worker, secretary, sportswoman, mother, whore and all these rolled into one. And, where women are concerned, advertising has to focus on the feelings they arouse.

For when it comes to marketing, it is not a woman herself who counts, but the fantasy that the male or female audience entertains about her. "Between fantasy and its market value, cash, as one sign of the inestimable value of fantasy, forms an integral part of the representative mode of perversion." Thus Pierre Klossowski in his book, *La Monnaie Vivante* (Living Currency), whose evocative title directly relates to our subject. In other words, thanks to the advertising industry, women sell other women the means to sell themselves. "There are women who contrive to sell in themselves what would have found no takers if freely offered," said Stendhal mischievously. He is echoed by that odious misogynist Nietzsche, who stated: "No-one wants her for free, what else can she do but sell herself!"

Eve's apple – talky and silent underwear

The admen have thus had to put all their intuition, cunning, research and marketing techniques into recovering the original secret: how was Eden's apple sold? In their view, lingerie is primarily the story of an eye looking at an eye looking at an undergarment. The eye belongs, of course, to the woman checking, first in the eyes of other women, and then in men's eyes (men being, after all, her primary objective) whether she has a "good eye" for these matters. And since we are all fetishists at heart, the advertising industry has also become fetishist. It has been known for years that Italian men are more interested in child-bearing hips (the Italian "Mama"), that Frenchmen are more susceptible to shapely legs, and that British and American men, probably still nostalgic for their infancy, are fixated on heavy, swollen breasts. There is a world of difference between the German school (prominent Valkyrie-style bust), the Italian school (low breasts, like a she-wolf's) and the French school (breasts forming "Golden Triangles" between collarbone and nipples).

The film industry is our barometer. It provides an accurate reflection of the latest trends in lingerie fashion and the fetishes that these generate. The emphasis is placed by turns on shoulders, breasts or legs. In the period before talking pictures, the spotlight was on the legs, preferably sheathed in silk. In the heyday of the talkies, Mae West and her famous corset launched the fashion for callipygous women. After the Second World War, the emphasis shifted to breasts, beginning with the film *The Outlaw,* which starred Jane Russell in the bra designed by Howard Hughes, the ancestor of today's "Wonderbra". Then came the era of Marilyn Monroe's knickers, glimpsed when she stood over the hot air vent and famously placed in the refrigerator when the summer was hot (legend has it that she only ever wore knickers when filming). After this came the era of the waif-like Twiggies, the anorexics, Brigitte Bardot's tights, and so on. Today, the organ favoured by the film industry is not named. Many taboos have fallen by the wayside and advertisers are perfectly happy to reveal nipples, the cleft of the buttocks or pubic hair showing through the fabr￼ But advertisers, as opposed to film-makers, know how to remain "soft" because they have to stay in the game. The "harder" things get, the more difficult it is to find something new.

Under Cinderella's skirts

But can any man, even an adman, claim to fathom the mysterious workings of a woman's mind, her highly personal brand of logic, her deep-seated and innermost urges? One of these admen, Jean-Michel Goudard, admits his limits: "Helpless and ineffectual, I allowed the woman symbolising Chantelle lingerie to lead the life of a chameleon. One day chaste, the next promiscuous, a sportswoman here, a society lady there… And we never knew if our Chantelle woman was chaste, frivolous, liberated or merely practical." The manufacturers association has even created a special category, wittily dubbed the "double agent";

this is the Sloane-Ranger-type woman who secretly wears a black suspender belt, like those favoured by call-girls, under her Chanel suit.

Inside every advertising executive is a fairy godmother waiting to get out, ready to help Cinderella go to the ball. But, other days, other ways; in the past, the posing Cinderella seemed quite unaware that her clothes were missing. Now, on the contrary, suspender-belt-wearing models look as if they scarcely take them off for the shower. Striptease schools teaching wives how to undress seductively and thus reawaken their husbands' ardour are on the increase. The wives can mail-order the appropriate lingerie from glossy catalogues which arrive spontaneously with the post. Despite its vicissitudes, lingerie has risen again and again from its ashes, never ceasing to amaze. Haute-couture now proposes "underwear" as "outerwear". Dresses are made using "waspies", half-cup bras and waist-clinchers. Corsets and embroidered petticoats have become the key components of modern two-pieces or trendy evening dresses. It is probably only a matter of time before a pair of knickers is worn as a hat! Mirroring the development of sexuality, lingerie has continued its course into the once private, but now increasingly popular, domain of SM (Sado-Masochism). The French fashion house, Demonia, sells astounding underwear in leather or vinyl. These garments lend themselves, at clubs or in private, to the most risqué performances and an infinite variety of sexual activities.

A redoubtable weapon

Lingerie is not simply a matter of taste. For women, it has everything to do with instinct and sensitivity, fundamentally feminine qualities. Men who love women, and know a little about their intimate relationship with lingerie, cannot help but join Jacques Laurent in his plea: "Because lingerie clings to the most secret, the most febrile, and, for men, the most thrilling parts of a woman's body… it allows the imagination to run riot . Women may be running a risk if they forget that lingerie is a unique weapon – unique because it is designed to please the man it strikes while arousing in him the desire to strike back."

Lingerie
through the Ages

*"God made food,
the devil the cooks."*
JAMES JOYCE

◄ Lucas Cranach: *Adam and Eve.* 1526
▶ *Eve.* Drawing by René Giffey. 1930

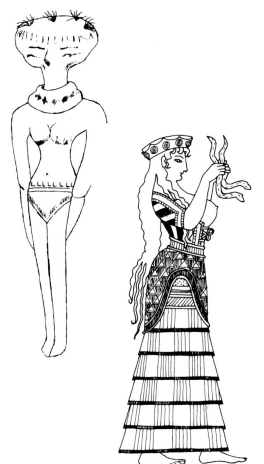

▲ The first *pair of briefs*. Sumeria. 3,000 BC

▶ The first *corset* – designed to accentuate Cretan women's proud breasts – and the first *crinoline* – which served only to emphasise their hips. Crete. 2000-1700 BC

Most Egyptian women wore nothing under their veils or tunics. However, slaves, dancing girls and prostitutes wore a tiny *G-string* (left page: Fresco from Pompeii.
Top left: Tomb of Djeserkaresonb, Thebes). Women athletes wore the precursor of the *bikini* (Mosaics from a Roman Villa. Below right: Atalanta wearing the *first modern undergarment.*)
Circa 1400-500 BC

Bra and *briefs* worn by female athletes. The Piazza Armerina Villa. 400-300 BC

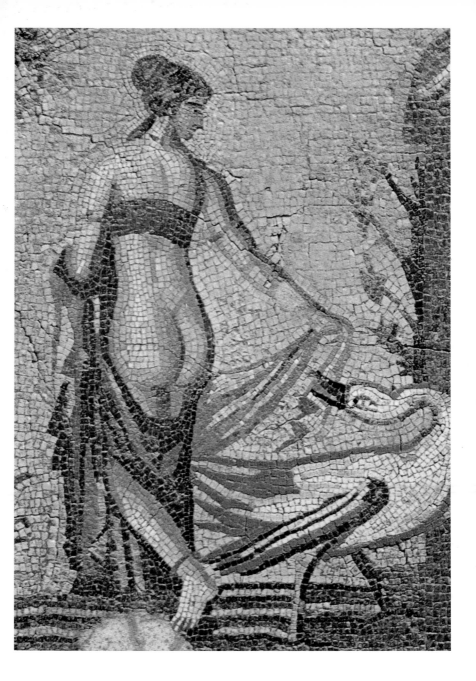

Cyprus. 300 BC

▲ 16th century. German caricature: *Chastity belt*. Money can buy you
everything and unlock any treasure.
◄ By the Middle Ages, knickers had disappeared. *The Très Riches Heures du
Duc de Berry* (detail). 14th century

▲ *Portrait of Joan of Arc.* The Franco-Flemish school. 15th century. Influence of armour on women's underwear

▼ *French Farthingale,* a bell made of strips of wood or thick wire. Replaced in France by a *stuffed roll* or *"bum roll"* which held out the skirt. 1595

▲ Iron *"body"*. 16th century

▲ Whalebone *pannier*, designed to hold the dress out at the sides, making it more accessible. 16th century

▼ *Farthingale*, a lighter model made of wood and ties, France. Late 16th century

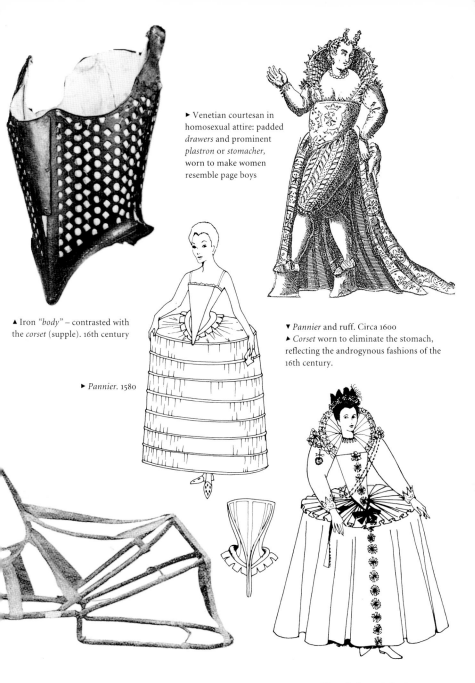

▶ Venetian courtesan in homosexual attire: padded *drawers* and prominent *plastron* or *stomacher*, worn to make women resemble page boys

▲ Iron *"body"* – contrasted with the *corset* (supple). 16th century

▶ *Pannier.* 1580

▼ *Pannier* and ruff. Circa 1600
▶ *Corset* worn to eliminate the stomach, reflecting the androgynous fashions of the 16th century.

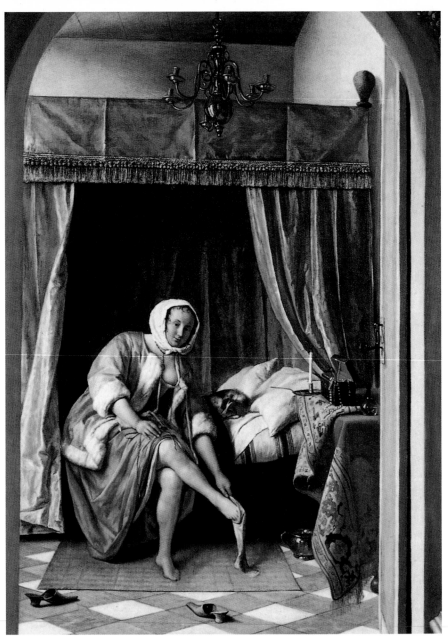

Wool or silk stockings first appeared in 1527 in England with the advent of the knitting machine. They immediately gained pride of place in the erotic fantasies generated by lingerie.
▲ Jan Steen: *The Morning Toilet* (detail). 1663   ▶ Nicolas Bernard Lépicié: *Fanchon Rising*. 18th century

Boned *stays*. 17th century

Corset. 1780

◄ François Boucher: *The Toilet* (detail). 1742

Dressmaker fitting *a pair of stays*. 1778

◄ *The Seamstresses* (detail). Late 18th century

► Jean Honoré Fragonard: *The Swing* (detail). 1766. A young nobleman gazing at the undergarments revealed by his mistress who, at that time, would not have worn any knickers. Note the young lady's erect little finger and her shoe, which has, like propriety, been thrown to the winds.

▼ Dressmaker and her *panniers.* 1778

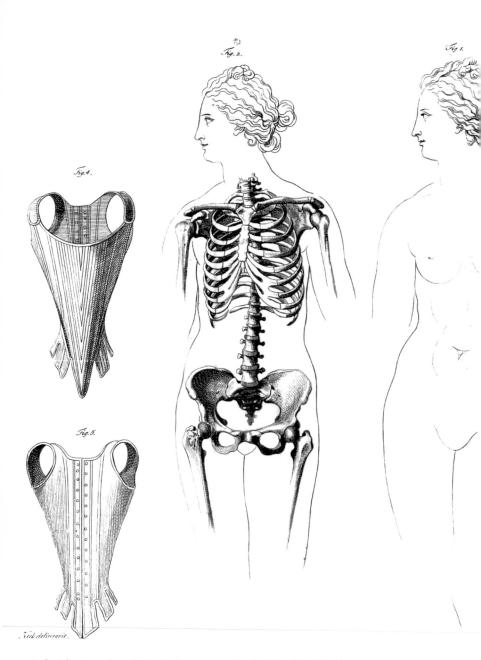

In the 18th century, the medical profession rose up against the deformities inflicted by corsets on the internal organs and skeleton of fashionable women. The requirements of fashion often proved fatal.

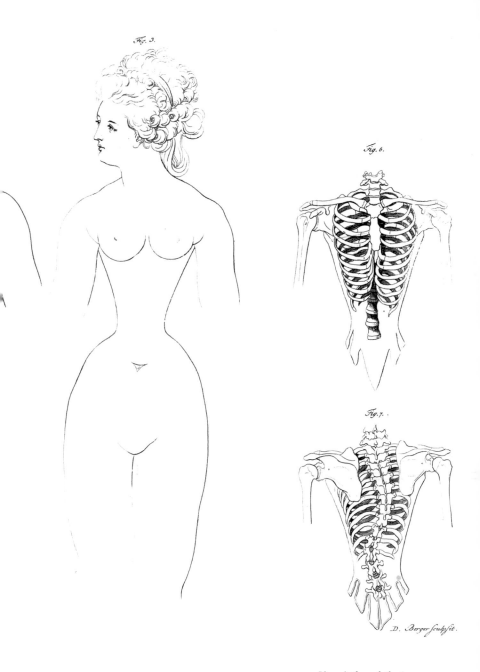

Fig. 3.

Fig. 6.

Fig. 7.

D. Berger sculpsit.

The Duchess at her Toilet. 18th century

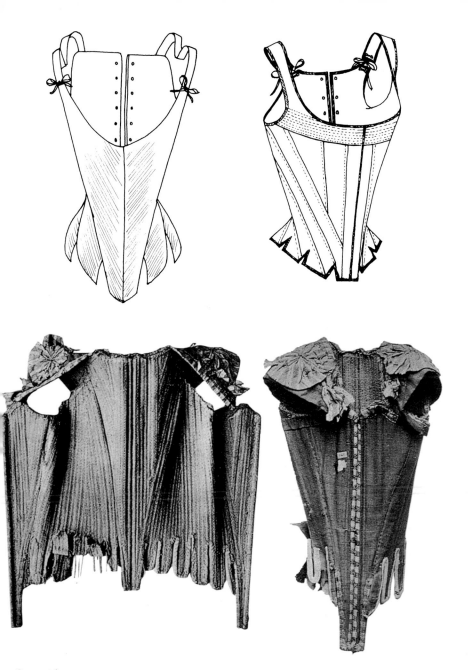

▲ *Corsets.* 18th century
▼ Open and laced *corset.* 1750

Panniers. 18th century. Line drawings by Jean Weber for Elizabeth Ewing's *Fashion in Underwear.*
B. T. Batsford Ltd. London. 1971

Richard Newton: *Pants.* 1796. A victory for women in the 18th
century. Until that time, *pantaloons* had only been worn by men.

Thomas Rowlandson: *A Little Tighter.* 1791

▼ The art of bust improvement. 1791
▲ "Beautiful Bosoms" *corset.* 18th century

Patent for *armoured undergarments* to protect women from being pricked by passing sadists in the street.

▲ *Modesty Betrayed.* Caricature from the
French Directory period. Circa 1816

▶ Vernet: *Parisian Fashions.* Circa 1800

CRIN

1

(Voir,
l'amusai
Albert
H
crino

P

La femme : vue extérieure

D'après une terre cuite co
(On en rencontre, quelquefois enc

The *crinoline* in 1850. Or the art of concealing your lovers

LINE

3

e sujet,
aquette de
Fizelière :
de la
u temps
.

350)

La femme : coupe intérieure
de la fin du second Empire
ez les raccommodeurs de faïences)

▲ "Windy Day" *crinoline*. English caricature. 1860
▶ A woman needed several helpers when putting on a *crinoline*. And would the doors be wide enough? Circa 1850

The opponents of the crinoline have fun in this comic strip suggesting unusual uses for the monstrous device. In *La Vie Parisienne*. 1860

CRINOLINE !!!!!

Nouvelle application de la Crinoline par les émules de Gérard.

La lune rousse

Sequel to the adventures of the Second Empire *crinoline*. In *La Vie Parisienne*. 1860

Parole d'honneur cher ! nos dames ont de toilette curieuse.

Supplice de Tantale

◄ Atget: *The Crinoline Shop*. Circa 1880   ▲ The wasp-waist. Circa 1893   **Lingerie through the Ages   58 · 59**

Nadar: *Woman in a Corset.* Circa 1890

The drawing in the centre reads:

A HISTORY OF THE CORSET

From 1902 to 1918, thousands of erotic postcards fuelled men's fantasies with pictures of the corset in every shape and colour. The drawing in the centre appeared in *Bizarre* in the 1950s

Lingerie through the Ages 60 · 61

1750   A. Baudoin: *The Toilet*

1830   *Slender waist*, lace three ells long

1900   A complicated exercise

1912   The *Amincis-sant*, the *Serpentin*, or the advent of stretch fabrics

1870 *Corset* for a *crinoline*

1890 The *chemise* eased the tortures of the *corset*

1925 The *corset* becomes a music-hall accessory

1948 The *waspie* by Marcel Rochas has replaced the corset

Lingerie through the Ages 62 · 63

▲ *Corseted Beauty.* In *La Vie Parisienne.* 1902   ▶ Edouard Manet: *Nana.* 1877

▲ Anonymous: *Tacit Consent.* Circa 1900
◄ Toulouse-Lautrec: *Conquête de passage (Casual Conquest;*
detail), woman wearing a corset for *Elles.* 1896 **Lingerie through the Ages 66 · 67**

LA BELLE SOPHIE.

Reutlinger: Portraits of late nineteenth-century beauties, Sophie, Bardou, Simier, dancing to the tune of "Who will dare to look at my legs?". Circa 1890

Following pages: The famous "5 demi-vièrges". Circa 1890

Toulouse-Lautrec's companions at the Moulin Rouge.
▲ Nini Pattes-en-l'air ► La Goulue. 1887

More of Toulouse-Lautrec's girlfriends in Montmartre.
◄ Grille d'égout   ▲ L'Hirondelle

Underwear worn by prostitutes in the brothels during the Second Empire and the reign of Queen Victoria.
Following pages: All manner of *"falsies"*. In *La Vie Parisienne*. 1881

s ces jolies petites mèches frisées ou ondu-
ondes, brunes, rousses ou noires, qui voir-
ront, sont montées sur un tulle rose qui
raie; de cette façon, on se pose ça sur le
la tête, on l'attache solidement et on peut
vent et l'humidité, rien ne bouge: frisure
e garantie! la pluie fait boucler davan-

On fait les mêmes fronts non
frisés; une bonne frange
droite, à l'usage des personnes
qui trouvent leur raie légitime
trop large ou leur frange pas
assez fournie. Rien de plus
gentil, du reste, que ces petits
toupets qui imitent le vrai à
s'y méprendre.

LA MÈCHE FOLLE. — Rebelle,
indisciplinée, taquine, revient
sans cesse sur le front, sur
les yeux, de façon à occuper
l'attention et faire dire:
« Cette mèche est insuppor-
table, elle est d'une nature
particulière, rien ne peut la
faire tenir ». La mèche folle
doit être montée sur une épin-
gle à branche torse, avec
agrafe de sûreté; la qualité
des cheveux doit être excep-
tionnellement remarquable.
Elle est destinée à être tou-
chée, baisée et quelquefois
même coupée par une main
émue et tremblante de bonheur.

LA GARNITURE. — Une forêt de cheveux souples, doux et
brillants, légèrement ondulés et bouclés du bout, pas trop
longs pour plus de vraisemblance, montés sur un large
ruban qui se coud à l'intérieur du chapeau d'amazone. Fait
très bien aux bains de mer, aux Pyrénées : même au
Bois, après le Grand Prix. On dit : « C'est ridicule de monter
à cheval avec les cheveux flottants », mais c'est pour les
reposer pendant l'été, et les naïfs de s'extasier. Par exemple,
ne pas accrocher son chapeau à une
branche et se mêler du vent dans l'avenue de l'Impératrice.

A FAUSSE POITRINE. — Deux demi-sphères de caoutchouc
et indore; suit admirablement les mouvements de
espiration, se redresse au toucher; est, sans contredit,
qu'on n'est pas dans l'intimité absolue, l'illusion est com-
Se fait aussi en satin ouaté et parfumé; plus agréa-
au porter, mais moins adhérent que le caoutchouc.

LA... CROUPE DE CAOUTCHOUC. — Remplace
avantageusement la « tournure » qu'elle est
en train de détrôner. Se fait en deux parties;
le caoutchouc doit être ferme, ne pas trop se
prêter. Charmant pour voyager sur une ban-
quette mal rembourrée ou monter un cheval
dur. Très pratique pour tomber sans douleur
au patinage. Produit au toucher une illusion
réelle. Se fait en caoutchouc plein et en caoutchouc soufflé; choisir de préférence le plein,
parce que ce soit un peu plus lourd, parce que
quelquefois un des côtés de l'autre système se
dégonfle brusquement et ça produit un effet
bizarre, surtout si l'on est à cheval ou en costume de bain.

LE FAUX VENTRE. — Un soupçon,
seulement, pour avoir l'air dessiné;
car s'il n'est pas joli d'avoir un ventre
saillant, il est encore plus laid de
n'en pas avoir du tout. Il faut absolument rompre la ligne droite; le ventre est un léger sachet plat des côtés, un peu renflé du milieu, qu'il s'attache à la robe. On est sûr, de cette
façon, qu'il n'ira pas se promener ail-
leurs, ce qui est d'un effet désastreux.
Se fait en caoutchouc et absolument
vrai pour les bains de mer.

YVES & BARRET SC

LE ROSE des
des narines se
l'essence et dé
ries de toilett
résistent vic
plus répétés.

ALBÂTRE

MANTEAU DE ROI

« Une fois pour
« femmes, ne devrie
« la grâce qu'elles

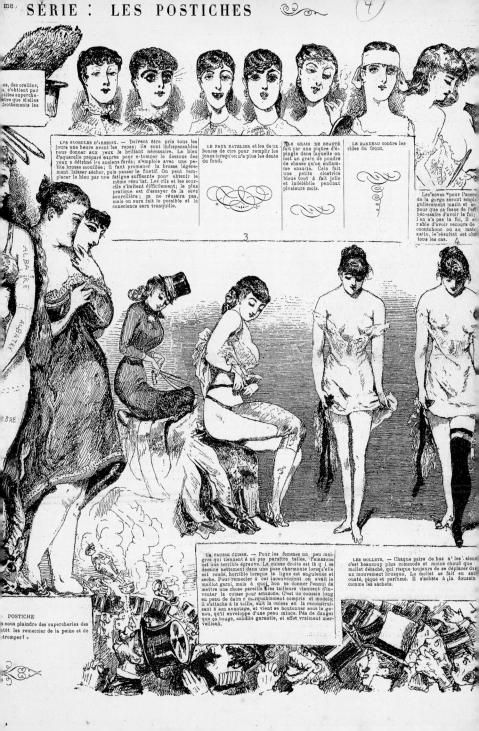

es, des oreilles,
a, s'obtient par
tites superche-
etre que si elles
frottements les

LES GLOBULES D'ARSENIC. — Doivent être pris tous les jours une heure avant le repas; ils sont indispensables pour donner aux yeux le brillant nécessaire. Le bleu d'aquarelle préparé exprès pour e-tomper le dessous des yeux a détené les anciens fards; s'emploie avec une pe-tite brosse mouillée; il faut promener la brosse légère-ment, laisser sécher, puis passer le fixatif. On peut rem-placer le bleu par une fatigue suffisante pour obtenir le même résu tat. Les cils et les sour-cils s'imitent difficilement; le plus pratique est d'essayer de la sève sourcillère; ça ne réussira pas, mais on saura fait le possible et la conscience sera tranquille.

LE FAUX RATELIER et les deux boules de cire pour remplir les joues lorsqu'on n'a plus les dents du fond.

LE GRAIN DE BEAUTÉ fait par une piqûre d'é-pingle dans laquelle on met un grain de poudre de chasse qu'on enflam-me ensuite. Cela fait une petite cicatrice bleue tout à fait jolie et indélébile pendant plusieurs mois.

LE BANDEAU contre les rides du front.

Les saves pour l'accro de la gorge seront emple-gulièrement mauis et so pour que ça fasse de l'eff néc-ssaire d'avoir la foi; l'on n'a pas la foi, il e rable d'avoir recours de caoutchouc ou au mate satin, le résultat est tous les cas.

3

LA FAUSSE CUISSE. — Pour les femmes un peu maigres qui tiennent à ne pas paraître telles, l'amazone est une terrible épreuve. La cuisse droite est q i se dessine nettement dans une pose charmante lorsqu'elle est ronde, horrible lorsque la ligne est anguleuse et sèche. Pour remédier à cet inconvénient on avait le maillot garni, mais à quoi bon se donner l'ennui de mettre une chose pareille les tailleurs viennent d'in-venter la cuisse pour amazone. C'est un cousin long en peau de daim r marquablement compris et modelé; il s'attache à la taille, suit la cuisse en la reconstrui-sant à son avantage, et vient se boutonner sous le ge-nou, qu'il enveloppe d'une peau mince. Pas de danger que ça bouge, solidité garantie, et effet vraiment mer-veilleux.

LES MOLLETS. — Chaque paire de bas a les siens c'est beaucoup plus commode et moins chaud que mollet détaché, qui risque toujours de se déplacer un mouvement brusque. Le mollet se fait en sat ouaté, piqué et parfumé. Il s'achète à la douzain comme les sachets.

POSTICHE
nous plaindre des supercheries des
tôt les remercier de la peine et de
tromper les

Honoré Daumier: *Outside the Corset-makers.* "Well I never, there's my wife!" 1840

American maternity corset. 1908

▲ American medical corset. Circa 1890   ▶ Atget: *Corsets on the Boulevard de Strasbourg.* 1909

Nº. 3. LE PANTALON BALLERINE.

Nº. 4. LE PANTALON DE DENTELLE.

Nº. 5. LE PANTALON-CHEMISE.

Nº. 6. LE PANTALON DE BRODERIE.

The allure of drawers. Girlie postcards from the 1900s

Nº 7. LE PANTALON D'ASSAUT.

Nº 8. LE PANTALON-COMBINAISON.

Nº 9. LE PANTALON DE SOIE.

Nº 10. LE PANTALON DE LA DANSEUSE.

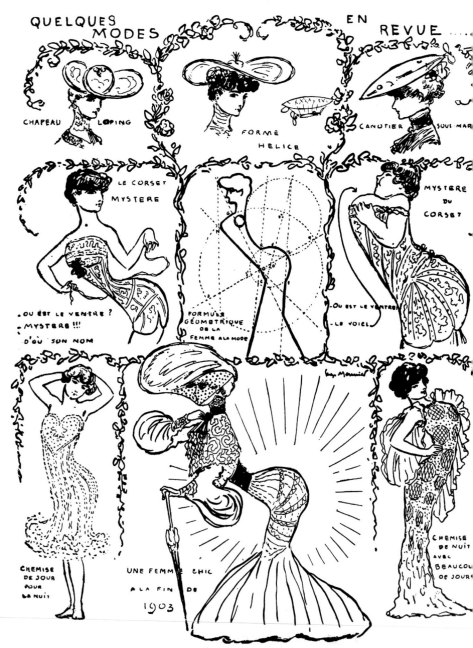

▲ G. Meunier: *Underwear and Outerwear* or geometry for fashionable women. "S" as in Sylphe. 1903

▶ Raphaël Kirchner: *The Elegant Corset* (Salon des humoristes). Circa 1900

▲ Edith la Sylphe, the monologuiste ► Her instrument, *the "Sylphide" corset*. Circa 1900

The art of lacing or unlacing *the "Sylphide" corset*. Circa 1900

Le but de cette manœuvre était d'allonger les bras (p. 147).

▲ Caricature by Esbey: *The Torture of Having Your Corset Laced or How to Lengthen Your Arms.* Circa 1900
▶ J. H. Lartigue: *Tram in New York.* Circa 1900. "Lower your skirts, ladies, you are showing your ankles."
Ankles and feet – which generated a new fetish for shoes – were all that could be seen of women in 1900.

▲ The *"Lysiane" corset* ◄ The "Pygmalion" range of designs at the Parisian department store, Bon Marché. 1891-1901

► The German *bust-improver* or a bust made to order

Gorgerette (Brusteinlagen)
aus Federfischbein.

Federleicht, luftig und sehr elastisch aus feinst. Seiden-Mousseline und durch Federfischbein in sinnreicher und praktischer Weise abgesteift.

Nr. 1

Nr. 2

Bequem und Hygienisch.

Unentbehrlich beim Tragen der modernen tailor-made Kleider.

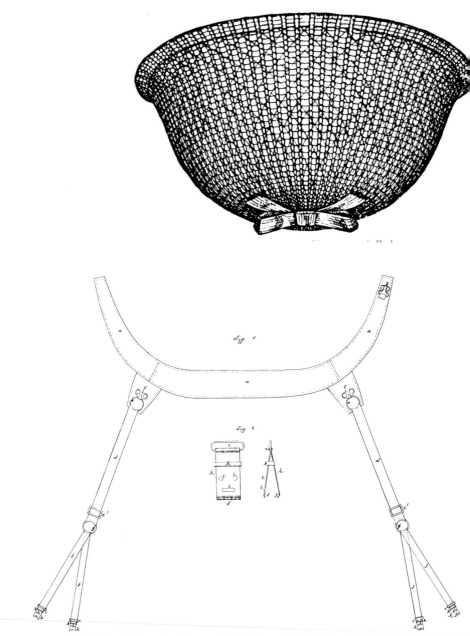

France can pride itself on the invention of the *suspender belt*. Patent by Fériol Dedieu. 1876. This invention has long been attributed to Gustave Eiffel, the architect of the Eiffel Tower in Paris, who, tired of seeing his wife's *stockings* twisted out of shape, reputedly made a *suspender belt* out of string and paper clips.

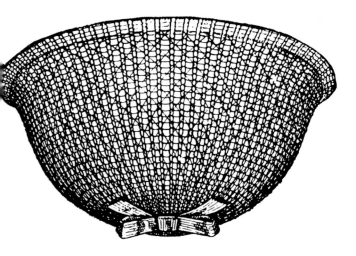

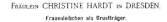

KAISERLICHES PATENTAMT.

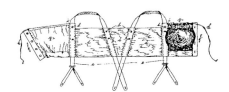

FRÄULEIN CHRISTINE HARDT IN DRESDEN.

Frauenleibchen als Brustträger.

PATENTSCHRIFT

— № 110888 —

KLASSE 3: BEKLEIDUNGSINDUSTRIE.

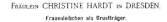

FRÄULEIN CHRISTINE HARDT IN DRESDEN.

Frauenleibchen als Brustträger.

Patentirt im Deutschen Reiche vom 5. September 1899 ab.

Das Frauenleibchen als Brustträger besteht aus Rücken- und Seitentheilen d, auf welche Schlaufen a aufgenäht sind, durch welche Männerhosenträger jeder Art (e) eingeführt und durch Knöpfe b befestigt werden können. Der Vordertheil ist in der Mitte bei f zusammenzuknöpfen. Zur Aufnahme je einer Brust sind Behälter g^1 und g^2 bestimmt, die unten und an der Seite fest umnäht sind, oben aber mit Band h, welches durch den Behälterstoff g^1 und g^2 geführt und am Ende i festgenäht ist. Bei g^1 ist ein aufs kleinste zusammengezogener Brustbehälter und bei g^2 ein solcher in größter Ausdehnung veranschaulicht.

Der Zweck dieses Leibchens besteht hauptsächlich darin, die Brüste aufrecht zu halten, ohne die Function einer gesunden Brust irgendwie zu beeinträchtigen. Dabei sind die Brustbehälter der jeweiligen Größe der Brust gemäß verstellbar.

Rücken und Seitentheil d dient nur dazu,

dem Leibchen einen Zusammenhalt zu geben, so daß es aus einem Stücke besteht, ist aber im Umfange so reichlich gehalten, daß beim Zuknöpfen durchaus kein festes Anliegen des Leibchens am Rücken und an den Seiten des Körpers entsteht, und es wird somit jeder gesundheitschädliche Druck auf die Brustorgane vermieden. Die Brüste werden nur in ihren anschliefsend stellbaren Brustbehältern mit Hülfe der Träger e hochgehalten, nicht aber durch ein fest um Brust und Rücken anliegendes Korsett oder Leibchen. Das Leibchen ist nicht fest mit den Trägern verbunden, sondern diese sind abknöpfbar, so daß das Leibchen bequem gewaschen werden kann.

PATENT-ANSPRUCH:

Frauenleibchen als Brustträger mit verstellbaren Brustbehältern, dadurch gekennzeichnet, daß dasselbe von seinem verstellbaren Träger behufs Waschens getrennt werden kann.

Hierzu 1 Blatt Zeichnungen.

Zu der Patentschrift

№ 110888.

▲ However, England must be credited with the invention of the first *bra*, probably dreamed up by a tea drinker obsessed with his tea strainer. Patent from 1886
▼ Several years later, Germany met this challenge and patented a more supple *bra*.

The *corset* worn for cycling. Photo from *Die Erotik in der Photographie*, 1898

► Minor inventions: the *corset with suspenders*, which had the advantage of
preventing the corset from riding up while also holding up the stockings. 1893

▲ Underwear worn on stage in 1900: a corseted diva. In *Visions d'art plastique*
▶ The *sexy corset*. In *La Vie Parisienne*. 1870. Founded in 1860, *La Vie Parisienne* was the original girlie

magazine. Thereafter, from *Pour Lire à Deux* (Reading for Two) to *Playboy*,
they all made extensive use of lingerie-clad models.

The underwear worn by the beauties of 1900 – here photographed by Reutlinger, a specialist in the genre – looked more like jewellery.

La Belle Otéro and her *suspender belt* made in precious stones by the
jeweller Boucheron during the reign of Napoleon III.

LA VIE PARISIENNE

LA DAME AUX MASQUES

▲ The last bulwark of modesty, the *body stocking*, the precursor of *tights*, made its appearance worn by strippers, actresses and dancers. 1910s

◄ *Body stockings* became more sheer and see-through in the 1920s. Cover of *La Vie Parisienne*. 1927

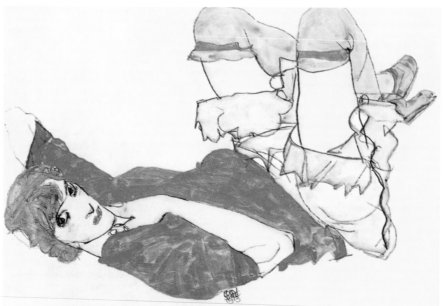

Egon Schiele went to prison for drawing very young girls wearing only their underwear at "play". 1913-1918

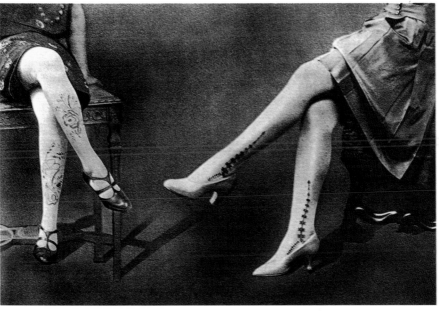

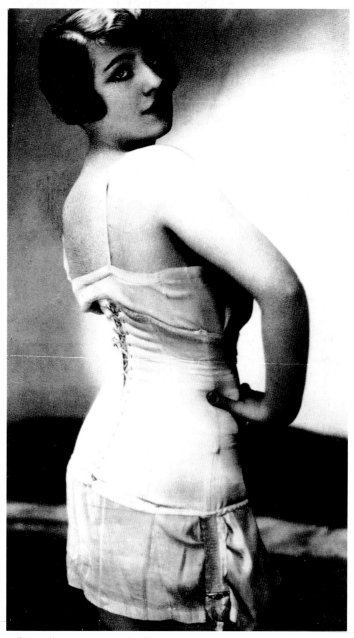

▲ The *corset* became emancipated and less constricting.
▶ The *corset* also became retro in style, worn by dominant women. Here Yva Richard. 1920s.
Collection belonging to Alexandre Dupouy, author of *Yva Richard – L'âge d'or du fétichisme*. 1994

Yva Richard also featured as the "trade mark" of a shop near the Opéra in Paris which, in the 1920s, sold sexy lingerie and was visited in secret by daring middle-class women. One of the first mail-order organisations, it sent out fetishist catalogues which showed the voluptuously underclad Yva as soubrette, exhibitionist, sailor, rider and school girl – catering, in short, for all tastes. Alexandre Dupouy Collection

C. Hérouard: Drawing for "Their Knickers" series. 1920s. The advent of a less restrictive fashion encouraged the return of the chemise.

J. H. Lartigue: *Bibi at the Hôtel des Alpes*, Chamonix. 1920
Camiknickers made of pleated crêpe de Chine.

C. Hérouard: Drawing for "Their Knickers" series: *Satan's Sarabande.* 1920s

The dispute between "restrictive" (left) and "loose-fitting" (right) styles.
Women liberated themselves from their straitjackets and conservative
women were horrified, England. 1928

The Three Graces sporting the newfangled *suspender belts*, England. 1928

C. Hérouard: Illustration for "Their Knickers" series:
Indiscretions of the Wind. 1920s

Silk *chemise* and *knickers*, France. 1925

▲ C. Hérouard, Drawing for "Their Knickers" series. 1920s
◄ *Knickers*, France. 1920

Loose-fitting styles dominated women's fashion during the Roaring Twenties: *stockings* and *négligée,* along with the inevitable cloche hat.

In the late 19th century, the *négligée* was a lightweight dressing gown or house coat which could be worn when entertaining close friends. Women of the Roaring Twenties made it into a completely frivolous undergarment.

115

Until the end of the 1920s, the *negligée* or *déshabillé* remained – with *stockings* – the sexiest piece of lingerie in a woman's wardrobe. This was because the women who wore them looked as if they were indeed *déshabillées:* all but nude.

Photos Schall for the girlie magazine *Pour Lire à Deux*. 1936. In the 1930s, women had become more liberated, but felt a certain nostalgia for the clinched waist of the sadomasochistic 1900-style *corset*.

Vogue endorsed the new fashion, inspired by Antiquity, of corseted Caryatids. But the *corset* was now elastic, supple and without laces. 1934

Horst P. Horst: *Corset* for *Vogue*. 1939

Alfred Eisenstaedt: *Girdles for the Fuller Figure*. Germany. 1937. The advantages of stretch fabrics.

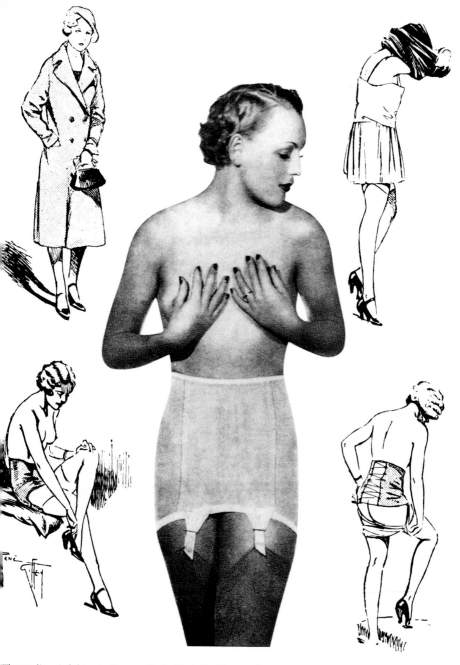

The new lingerie fashions in the 1930s: the *flexible girdle with suspenders.*
Sketches by René Giffey.

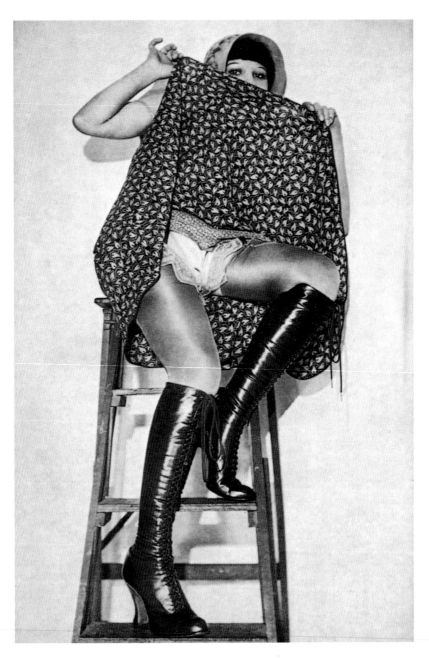

Another star of the 1930s: *briefs*, which women were no longer ashamed to reveal when climbing a stepladder or getting on a swing.

Briefs in all shapes and sizes
▲ Vasta Images-Books. 1930
▶ Jean Dulac: Drawing for *Les Dessous d'un demi-siècle*. 1956

The spirit of the 1930s recreated in 1953 by a nostalgic Man Ray. He entitled his photo *Lassitude*.

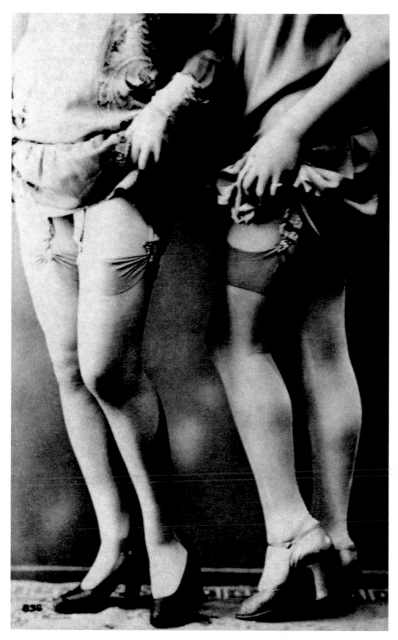

But the great success story of the 1930s was, more than ever, *stockings* and their counterpart, the *suspender belt,* without which the *stockings* would not stay up. These two garments epitomised the allure of lingerie, which was seen everywhere, even on the silver screen.

Laure Albin-Guillot: *Stockings* series. 1930s. A woman photographing
the feminine appeal of lingerie.

Laure Albin-Guillot: *Stockings* series. 1930s

▲ Jean Dulac: *The Flappers.* Drawing for *Les Dessous d'un demi-siècle.* 1956
▶ 1925 also marked the advent of the flapper. She wore her hair bobbed and borrowed men's clothing, but retained the

good old blackstocking look. Here, the writer Colette, when she was making her debut at the BA.TA.CLAN in the revue *Ça grise*. 1930s

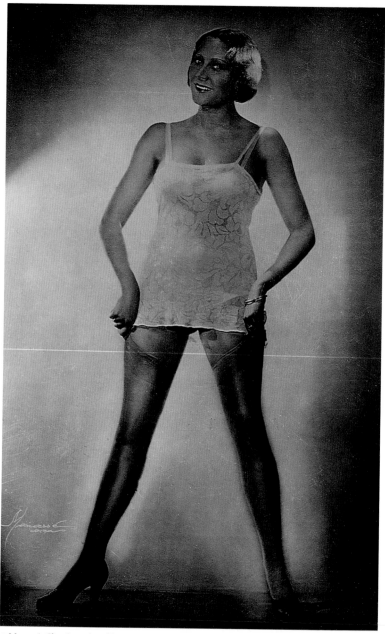

▲ Manassé: *Chemise* and *stockings*. 1930   ▶ Jean Dulac: Drawing for *Les Dessous d'un demi-siècle*. 1956
Following pages: A woman's complete outfit 1925-1930: bobbed hair, *chemise*, wide *suspenders* and *stockings*, shoes with straps

The modern woman coming to grips with a new rival, the motor car. Circa 1927

▼ Drawing by Giffey: *The Breakdown.* 1930s

In France, paid holidays entered the law in 1927. Freed from work, women escaped into the countryside. There they rode bicycles and rowed boats, treating all and sundry to a view of the underwear and

suspenders beneath their flimsy dresses. Postcards from the time.

Lingerie out in the open, enjoying paid holidays. Girlie postcards and drawings by Giffey. 1930s

Giffey: *The art of climbing trees.* 1930s
Dialogue: "Isn't climbing trees good for the health?" — "And the view!"

Anonymous: The art of crossing your legs in fashionable society to
show off your underwear to its best advantage. 1930s

Girls in films had been discovered by
Pour Lire à Deux, 1937; now you see them,
now you don't, a half-clothed bit part.

The triumph of *French knickers*, which allowed the air to circulate freely and put almost everything on display. *Sex Appeal.* 1936

The perfect secretary, according to *Pour Lire à Deux*. 1937

The vamp's underwear, according to the Hungarian photographer,
Manassé. Circa 1930. Note the thick silk *stockings* and the wide, eye-
catching *suspenders*.

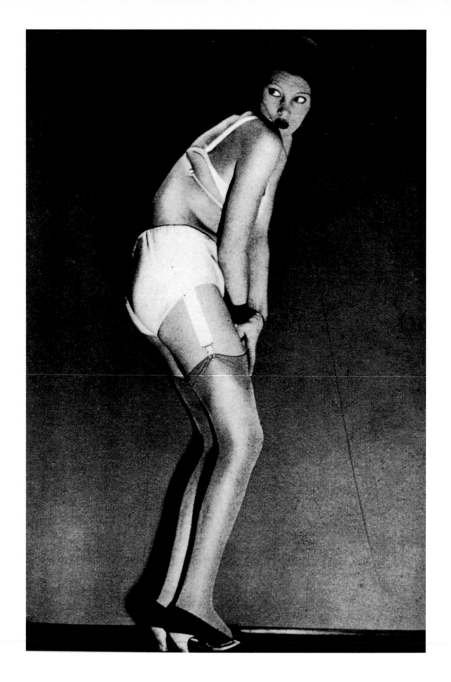

Schall: Diana Slip designs. 1932

Manassé: Typical 1930s-style lingerie worn by a nice, wholesome girl   **Lingerie through the Ages   162 · 163**

Manassé: The vamp's underwear in a post-cubist setting, Hungary. Circa 1930-1935

The New Look *waspie*, France.
1947

Marcel Rochas invented the *waspie*. 1945

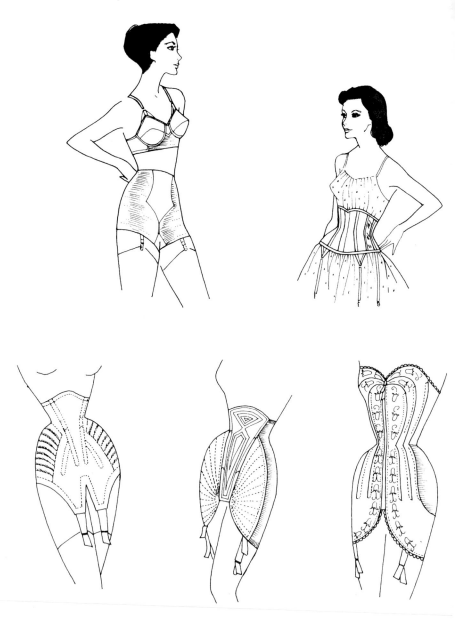

▲ New Look *corsets*, a subtle blend of nylon (a legacy from wartime parachutes) and satin (a legacy from our grandmothers). 1947-1948. Line drawings by Jean Weber for *Fashion in Underwear*.

▶ *Corselette.* 1947

Encouraged by the retro style of Christian Dior's New Look, the Diana Slip fashion house tempted its customers with equally retro designs. 1940s-50s

▲ *Stockings* promotion in a New York department store. 1950s
◄ Shadow show of a *suspender belt* striptease.

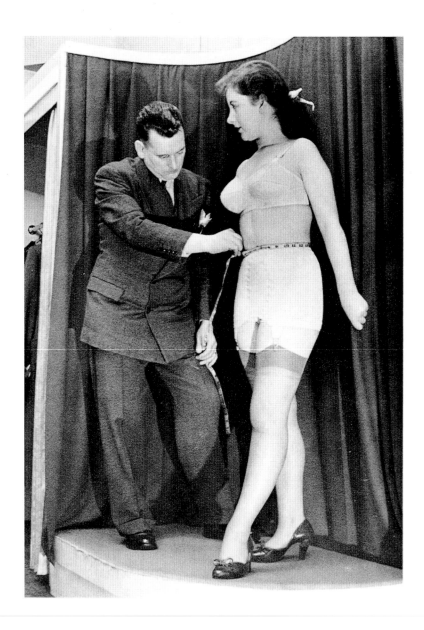

▲ Aubade makes the waist smaller, as proved by the tape measure. 1951
▶ *Corselette* by Marcel Rochas. 1952
▶▶ Swing in the beercellar nightclubs of Saint-Germain-des-Près. 1952

▲ Aubade catwalk parade. 1952
◀ The catwalk. *Vogue.* 1950s

▶ New Look
lingerie. 1948

After the Second World War, Europe was
impoverished and lacking in lingerie. But
business soon picked up. During the
rigours of rationing, women imitated
stockings with dye and *knickers* came to
resemble *G-strings*. The new taste for
luxury and opulence caused fashion to
revisit the past: the Belle Epoque, the
Roaring Twenties.

▲ Dress with matching *girdle,* Jean Patou. 1953

In 1945, Marcel Rochas, taking his inspiration from the old-fashioned *corset,* invented the *waspie* and, in 1947, Christian Dior took the world by storm with his famous New Look: slender waist, shapely bust and hips. Once again, the *corset,* or rather its modern replacements, the *girdle* or *waspie,* were essential for achieving this look, which was shown to advantage by a figure-hugging dress.

▲ Dior *corselette.* 1950

▲ Dress and matching *corselette,* Dior. 1950

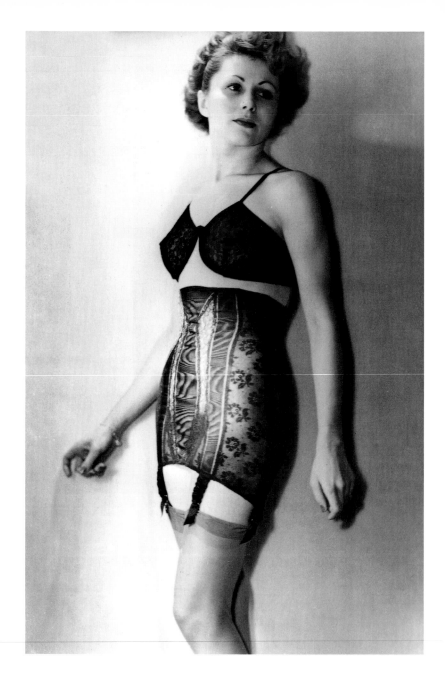

Styles from the Oriano range. 1951

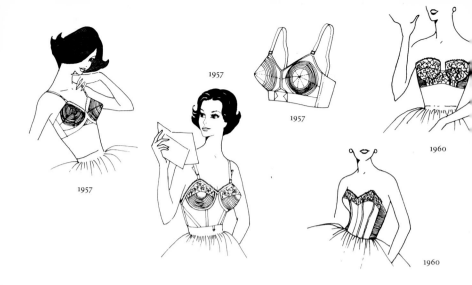

1957

1957

1957

1960

1960

1960

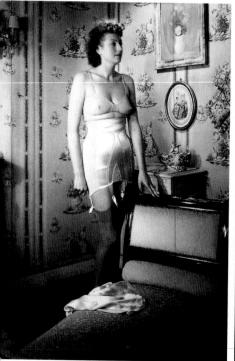

▲ Line drawings by Jean Weber for *Fashion in Underwear*. 1971
▼ Four Oriano designs. 1950-51

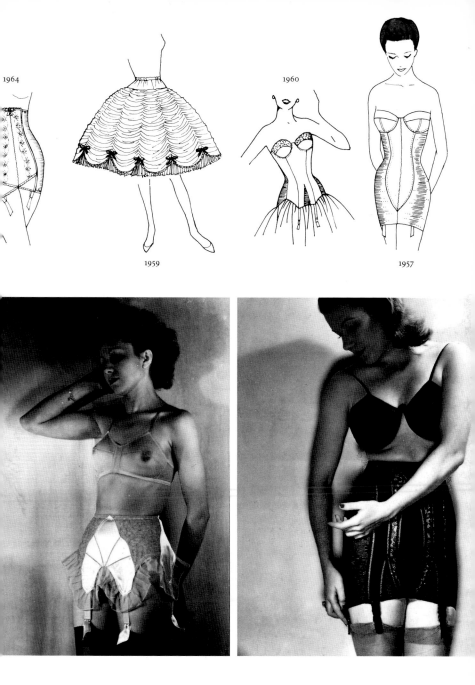

1964

1959

1960

1957

Lingerie through the Ages 182· 183

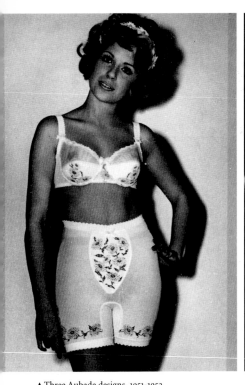

▲ Three Aubade designs. 1951-1952

1970

1960

1961

1963

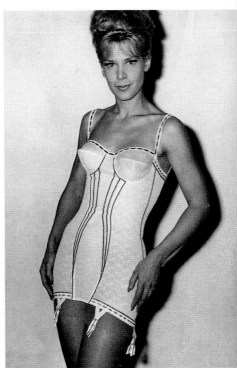

▼ Line drawings by Jean Weber for *Fashion in Underwear*. 1971

1958 1967

1967

A return to the eroticism of the French Belle Epoque. Triumph drew its inspiration from its 1886 collection to launch a range of historical styles made of new fabrics. 1950s

▲ American *fishnet tights.* Photo Fernand Fonssagrive. 1959
▶ Fishnet *body stocking,* USA. 1956

◄► *Hold-ups.* Germany. 1960s

▲ Le Bourget *hold-ups* and matching lingerie made of stretch Lycra lace, France. 1960s

Behind the scenes of a lingerie catwalk parade at the Stedelijk Museum. 1950s.
Underwear becomes highbrow.

he Corjoli *Jupant*. 1967. One-piece *panty girdle* and *slip*.

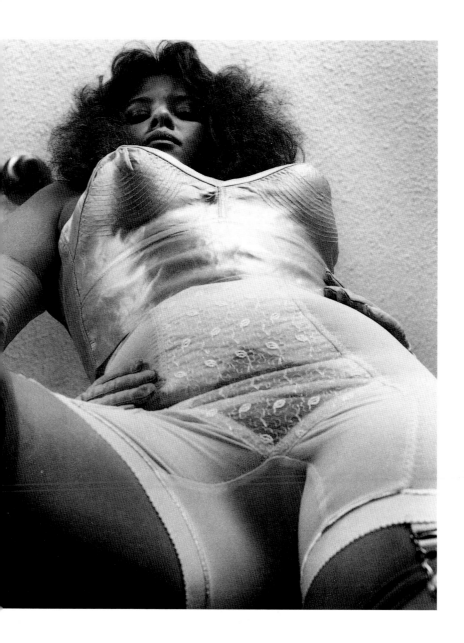

▲ The aggressive lingerie of the 1960s. Photo Eric Kroll
◀ Café-théâtre. 1968

A dazzling array of *panty girdles*. From left to right: Kaiser: *panty girdle* and matching *bra*. 1960s-70s. Aubade: two styles of *panty girdle* and *bra*. 1960s-70s. Model in her *panty girdle* waiting her turn in the catwalk parade. In *Vogue*. 1970s

In the 1960s-70s, loose-fitting
underwear again carried the day,
even if liberated women still
occasionally showed a certain
nostalgia for their former
straitjackets. Line drawings by
Jean Weber for *Fashion in
Underwear*. 1971

Women now seemed to have turned their back on restrictive undergarments. Lingerie show in 1970

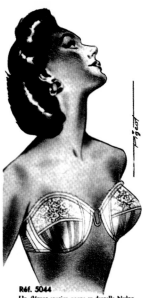

◄ Woman was now assembled from components: *bra, suspender belt, briefs.* Department store catalogue. 1970s

Réf. 5044
Un élégant soutien-gorge en dentelle Nylon doublée voile Nylon, avec bretelles amovibles, d'une adhérence totale, où le gansage du bonnet rehausse et maintient parfaitement la poitrine. Dos en tulle Lastex donnant le maximum d'aisance et de souplesse. Nouvelle armature flexplate garantie TARWIL, brevetée.

Réf. 244
Un porte-jarretelles en dentelle Nylon doublée voile Nylon, spécialement mis au point pour maintenir les bas bien à leur place.

NYLFRANCE

Réf. 1040
Le très seyant SLIP·LEJABY "ÉQUILIBRÉ" en dentelle Nylon doublée jersey Nylon, parfaitement étudié dans toutes les tailles pour donner le maximum de confort.

◄ The 1930s woman gazes at herself in the mirror, but in it sees a liberated, modern, almost naked woman self. Drawing by Solé. 1960s-70s

SOLÉ-KIRAT.

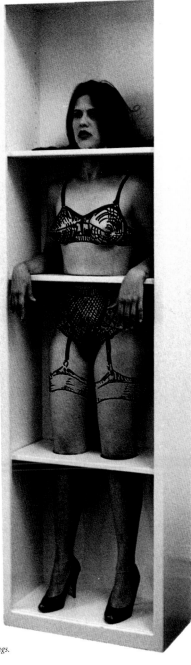

Components off-the-shelf in the 1970s. The missing piece: *stockings.*
hoto Eric Kroll, design Anna Noelle Rockwell

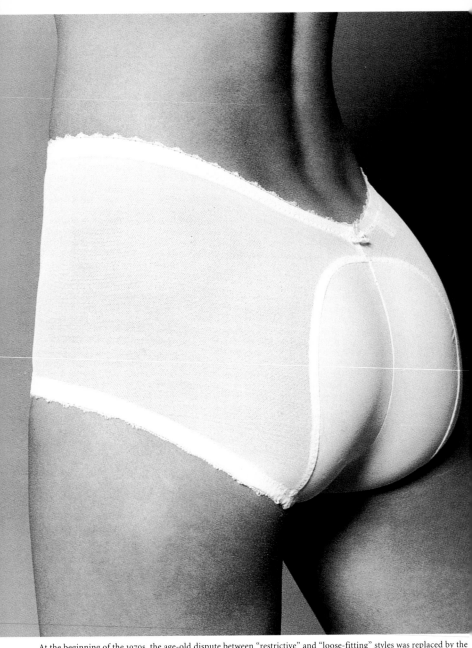

At the beginning of the 1970s, the age-old dispute between "restrictive" and "loose-fitting" styles was replaced by the dispute between "skin-tight" and "unfitted" styles. Here, an example of "skin-tight": stretch Lycra *panty girdle* with detachable *suspenders*.

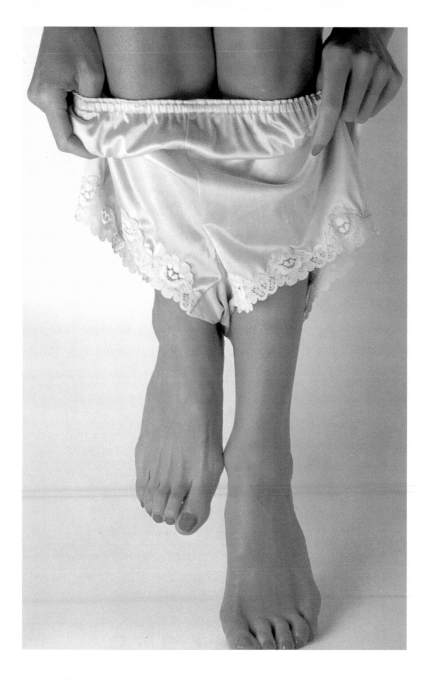

Example of "unfitted" *knickers.* 1960s-1970s

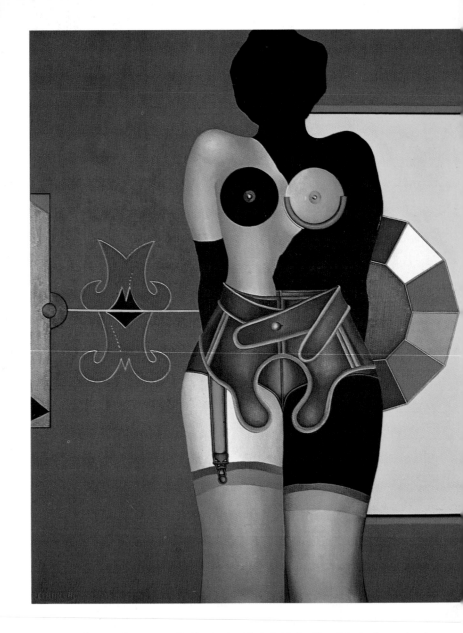

▲ Richard Lindner: *Marilyn Was Here. The Blue Angel* revisited, via Marilyn Monroe, by the German American pop artist, who specialised in "super-women" and their armour-like underwear.

▶ John Kacere: "Panties" series. 1971. Scanty diaphanous *briefs* perfectly depicted by a hyperrealist.

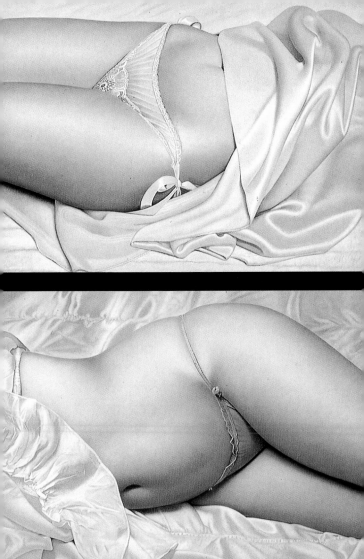

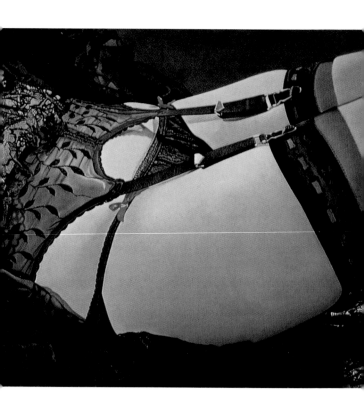

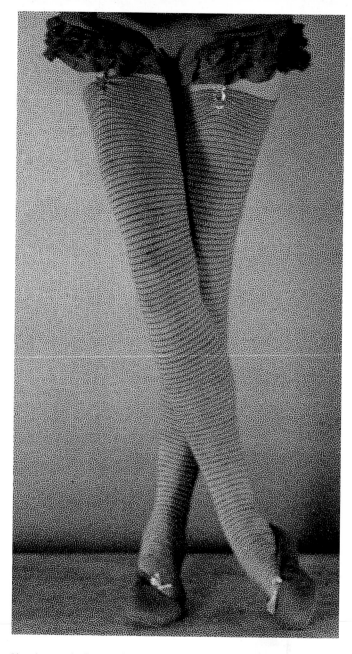

Lingerie as seen by the great photographers.
▲ Erwin Blumenfeld: *Jadis et Daguerre*. 1940s ▶ Jeanloup Sieff. 1985

Jeanloup Sieff: "Derrières" series ▲ 1985 ▶ 1996

Jeanloup Sieff: "Derrières" series. 1990

Jeanloup Sieff: "Derrières" series. 1990

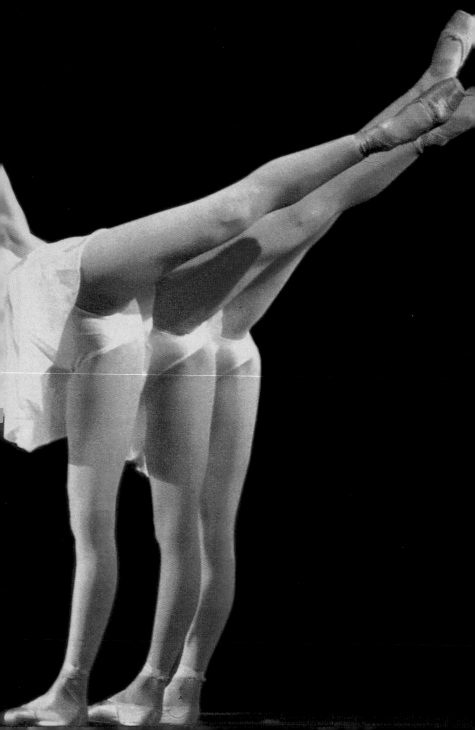

Dancers' underwear: *briefs* and *tights*

▲ Lucien Aigner: *At the Paris Opera*. 1950s ▼ E. Boubat: *Rear View of a Tutu*. 1950s

◄ The mandatory *knickers* worn by dancers since Louis XV.

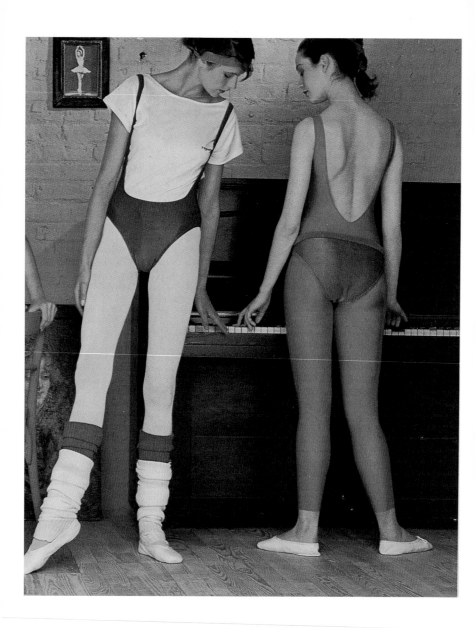

▲ Repetto: *Body stockings* in rehearsal. 1960s
▶ *Rehearsal at the Paris Opera.* It was Louis XV who decreed that dancers had to wear *tights* under their tutus. 1950s

Knickers for sportswomen. Wimbledon. 1960s

Jacques Henri Lartigue: *Woman Skiing.* 1940s

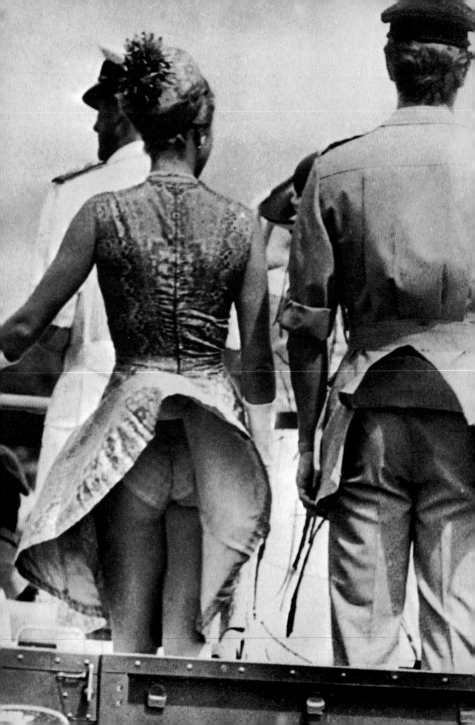

▲ Kurt Hutton: *Two at the Fair*. London. 1938
◄ *Knickers* worn by Princess Anne of England, indiscreetly
revealed by a gust of wind – to the delight of the paparazzi.

Lingerie through the Ages 222 · 223

▲ Dahmane: *The Revealing Corset.* 1985
▶ Cabaret theatre, Paris. 1973

Serge Jacques: *The Triumph of Lingerie.* 1980

Gilles Néret: *Lascivious Lingerie.* 1978

Women tend to waver between *suspender belts* and *tights*. Mail-order firms are aware of this, offering a wide range of choice, even a combination of the two. The key quality is eroticism. From left to right: *Fishnet tights,* leopard-skin print, *suspender belt style tights,* a compromise between the two, *lace suspender belt* and, the height of fetishism,

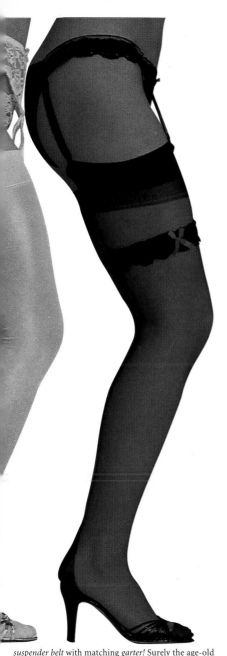

suspender belt with matching *garter!* Surely the age-old sight of a woman securing her stockings (far right) is not a thing of the past?

Previous pages:
Designs by Chantal
Thomass, a designer
who did much to
revive the popularity
of *stockings.* 1985

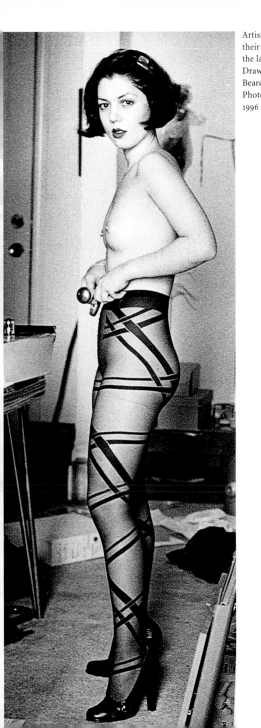

Artistic *tights* draw
their inspiration from
the last century.
Drawings by Aubrey
Beardsley. 1896.
Photos by Eric Kroll.
1996

▲ La Perla, embroidered *tights* made of stretch fabric. 1970. Publicity photo influenced by the "women-table" sculptures of Allen Jones
◄ Mary Quant, inventor of the miniskirt: Embroidered *tights*. 1965

▲ A veiled reference to the good old *corset,* with this *tights-and-corset* one-piece.
◄ The battle between function and erotic kitsch. 1972   **Lingerie through the Ages 236 · 237**

Between 1965 and 1970, *panty girdles* ousted the *corset,* and *tights* replaced the *suspender belt.* Colour was all important.
▲ *Panty girdles* made of Lycra, 9 colours, Printemps department store, Paris. 1967
▶ Jeanloup Sieff, publicity photo for Youpee *tights* from Dim. 1972

▲ Dim *tights* in 8 colours. 1971-1972 collection
◄ Embroidered *tights* by Chantal Thomass. 1970

Fishnet tights, **known in French as "fly-cage" tights, were once the hallmark of women of ill-repute. They are still in vogue today. 1980s**

Zoe Leonard: *Rear View*, catwalk parade in New York. 1990. All-enclosing *tights* captured by a fashion photographer. 1990s

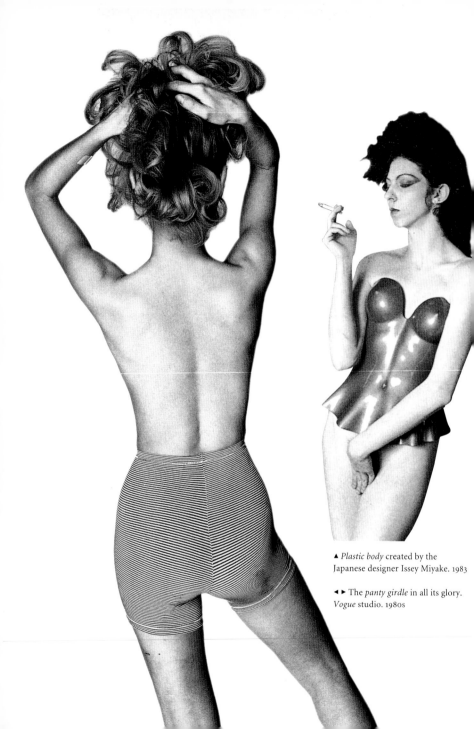

▲ *Plastic body* created by the
Japanese designer Issey Miyake. 1983

◄ ► The *panty girdle* in all its glory.
Vogue studio. 1980s

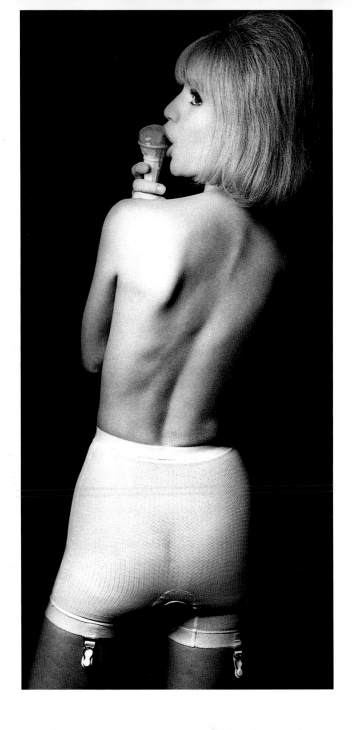

▲ Issey Miyake doubles as a sculptor with this *long-line bra* made of wire.
Photo Daniel Jouanneau. 1983
◄ Jeanloup Sieff, New York. 1962   **Lingerie through the Ages 246 · 247**

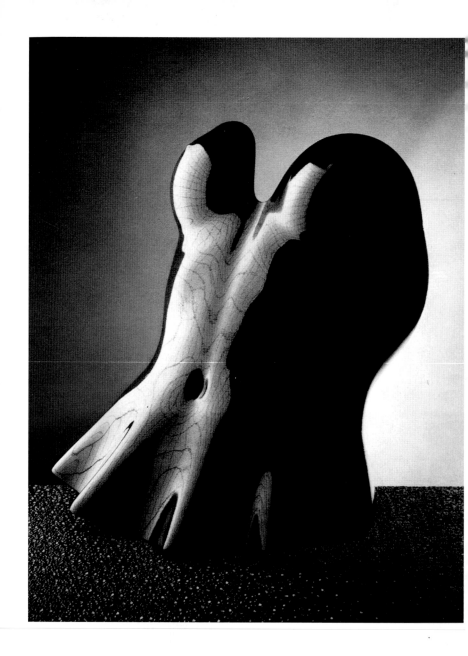

▲ Issey Miyake: *Plastic body.* 1983　▶ Pirelli calendar. 1973

Military-style catwalk parade or "Oh what a lovely war"
as seen by Chantal Thomass. 1984

A dazzling array of *waspies* in all the colours of the rainbow.
Chantal Thomass maintains a certain tradition. 1980s

Women go back to nature.
▲ The Natural Look, launched in New York in the 1980s ▶ Gemma lingerie set. 1985

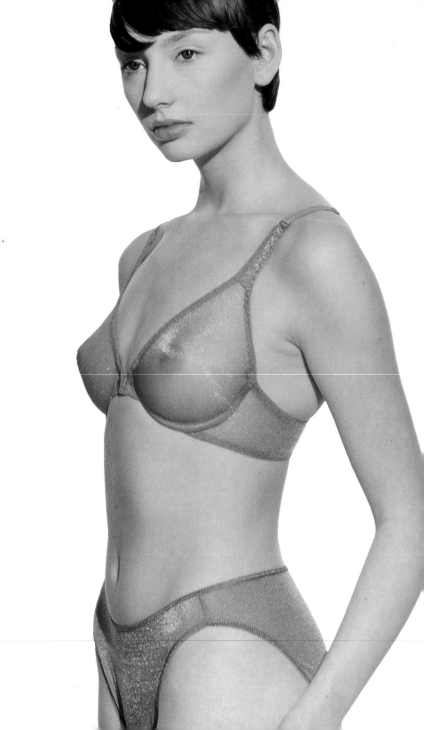

The next step after the Natural Look: see-through fabrics.
▲ In the 1990s, knickers became extremely brief, almost non-existent.
◄ Gossard sheer underwear. *Bra, bodysuit* and *briefs* have become invisible.

Say it with lace, because women will always want frills. Bottoms in luxury packaging. Bella, Turin. 1997

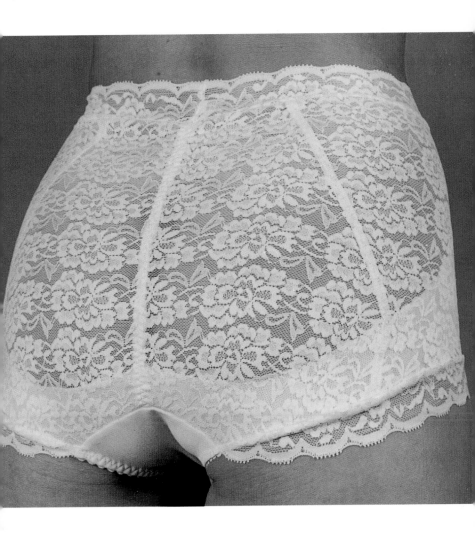

Luxury packaging for bottoms: feminine but a little kinky with provocative cut-outs. Also deceptive packaging, using padding to swell the truth. Bella, Turin. 1997

Underwear can no longer be ignored. Thanks to the leading couture houses, it has now been promoted to outerwear.
▲ Velda Lauder, London. Photo Robert Chouraqui. 1995
▶ Paco Rabanne: *Underwear-outerwear,* made of soft ostrich leather. 1993

From *Inside-Out,* the lingerie of the 1990s has become even more aggressive and shows SM tendencies. Demask, Amsterdam. Vinyl *corset.* Photo Robert Chouraqui. 1996

Pure, London: Matching vinyl *corset, knickers, suspenders* and boots.
Photo Robert Chouraqui. 1996

Mail-order sales of vinyl SM lingerie are steadily increasing.
Photos by Christophe Mourthé. 1998

Following in the footsteps of Mae West and Marilyn Monroe, Madonna enjoys shocking her audience by showing off her futuristic *corset*, with its pointed breasts shaped like live shells, designed for her by Jean-Paul Gaultier, and by throwing her *knickers* into the crowd… 1995

Lingerie
in Film

*"...legs sheathed
in their own venom..."*
JACQUES AUDIBERTI

◄ The striptease by Sophia Loren in Vittorio De Sica's
Yesterday, Today and Tomorrow. 1963

▲ Betty Boop and her *garter*. Comic strip
from the 1920s

Cinema is a barometer of women's underwear, charting its contemporary history. Theda Bara, Hollywood's first sex-goddess, in her oriental underwear in *Cleopatra*. 1917. Her agents claimed that she had ruined fifty men and broken up 150 homes.

Another of Hollywood's early sex symbols, Mae West. Her voluptuous curves and sexy *corset* shot her to fame and formed a welcome contrast to the skeletal flappers who were then in vogue. Here, in *Diamond Lil.* 1928

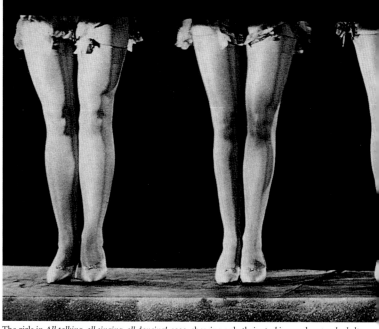

The girls in *All talking, all singing, all dancing!*, 1929, showing only their *stockings* and *suspender belts*.

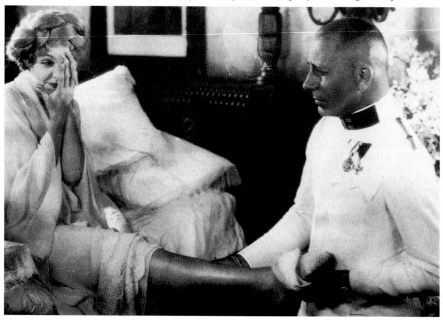

ZaSu Pitts mischievously hides her face, while Erich von Stroheim removes her stockings in his film *The Wedding March*. 1926

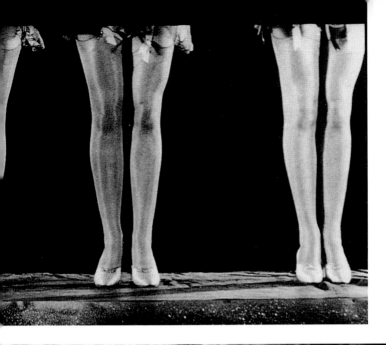

Marlene Dietrich, her "legs sheathed in their own venom" (Audiberti),
vamping it up in decadent Berlin for *The Blue Angel*. 1930

▲ The provocative *suspender belt* mark one: *The Blue Angel,*
by Josef von Sternberg, with Marlene Dietrich. 1930
◄ Marlene's sex appeal was regarded as so irresistible that Hollywood exploited it
to caricatural extent. *Golden Earrings* by Mitchell J. Leisen. 1947
Following pages: The vamp *par excellence* in the 1930s, Marlene, in *The Blue Angel*

The provocative *suspender belt* mark two: Liza Minnelli recreates
1930s Berlin in Bob Fosse's *Cabaret*. 1972

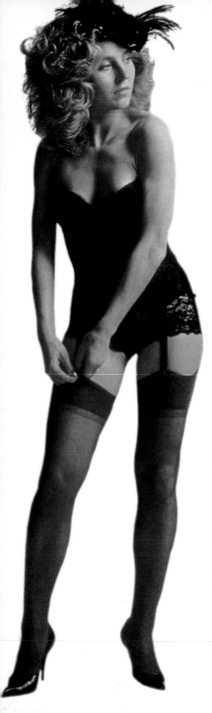

◄ The provocative *suspender belt* mark three: Hanna Schygulla in
The Marriage of Maria Braun by R. W. Fassbinder. 1978

► And its sequel, mark four: Barbara Sukowa,
in *Lola,* also by R. W. Fassbinder. 1981

R.W. Fassbinder

Où
se termine
LE MARIAGE DE
MARIA BRAUN
commence...

Lola

UNE FEMME ALLEMANDE

Rainer Werner Fassbinder ... Barbara Sukowa / Mario Adorf / Armin Mueller-Stah

▲ American burlesque of the 1920s. A good excuse for an eye-catching display of contemporary lingerie.
▶ Mervyn Le Roy: *The Gold Diggers of 1933*. 1933. The most effective tools for striking gold: *suspender belt* and *stockings*.

Following pages: *Too Much Harmony*. 1933. Cinema, in its early stages, made extensive use of women's underwear, following in the tradition of the "Coucher d'Yvette" of the last century.

1452-114

A WARNER BROS. & VITAPHONE PICTURE.

FASHIONS OF 1934

A WARNER BROS.
& VITAPHONE
PICTURE

42ND

STREET

WARNER BAXTER
BEBE DANIELS
GEORGE BRENT

UNA MERKEL · RUBY KEELER · GUY KIBBEE
NED SPARKS ● DICK POWELL
DIRECTED BY LLOYD BACON

▲ The film industry draws on the past, reviving the French Can-Can. Here, *Une nuit au Moulin Rouge*. 1950s
◄ "Fashions of 1934", or everything you ever wanted to know about 1930s underwear. *42nd Street* by Lloyd Bacon. 1933.
Another film that glorified the charms of underwear in dance numbers that were expressly included for this purpose.

▲ Shirley MacLaine dancing a frenzied French Can-Can in Walter Lang's *French Can-Can*. 1960s
► Gina Lollobrigida is equally wild in *La donna più bella del mondo* by Robert Z. Leonard. 1950s
Following pages: The dance number from *French Can-Can* by Jean Renoir. 1955

▲ *Moulin Rouge,* John Huston's life of Toulouse-Lautrec. 1953
► The harsh backstage life was (also) depicted by Bob Fosse in *All that Jazz.* 1979

Platinum blonde: Jean Harlow, the new vamp of the 1930s. Her black lace underwear contrasts strikingly with her hair. Publicity photo

The underwear worn by beautiful Southerners during the American Civil War:
Vivien Leigh being laced into her *corset* by her black nurse in *Gone with the Wind*
by Victor Fleming. 1939

Parisian lingerie
▲ Henri-Georges Clouzot: *Quai des Orfèvres*, with Suzy Delair and Louis Jouvet. 1947
◄ Arletty, in *camiknickers*, has her hand kissed by Dalio in *Tempête* by Bernard-Deschamps. 1939

Photo session, with provocative lingerie and lesbian overtones, between Suzy Delair (the model) and Simone Valère (the photographer) in *Quai des Orfèvres* by Henri-Georges Clouzot. 1947

The provocative *waspie* or the Italian bride's underwear
▲ Rosanna Schiaffino, in *Arrivederci, Baby* by Ken Hughes. 1966
▶ The *waspie* worn by Yoko Tani in *Paris-Canaille.* 1950

Ginette Leclerc's brief, chance meeting at the "L'Hôtel du libre échange", a farce by Georges Feydeau, adapted by Jacques Prévert, who also wrote the dialogue, and directed by Marc Allégret. 1934

A beautiful courtesan, sheathed in lace and nylon: Silvana Pampanini
wreaked havoc in *The Woman Who Invented Love* by Ferruccio Cerio. 1952

The sexy black cotton *stockings* worn by Italian peasant women working in the rice fields.
▲ Elsa Martinelli in *The Rice Field* by Raffaello Matarazzo. 1956
▶ Silvana Mangano in *Bitter Rice* by Giuseppe De Santis. 1949

Underwear and bestiality
Betty Grable and her bear in *Meet Me After The Show* by Richard Sale. 1951

Johnny Weissmüller, alias *Tarzan, the Ape Man,* by W. S. van Dyke, 1932, keeping watch over his woman, Maureen O'Sullivan, who models a pelt two-piece.

**C'EST
PARIS**

▲ Martine Carole performing in a circus in retro-style underwear in *Lola Montès*
by Max Ophüls. 1955
◄ And wearing a *waspie* on the cover of a girlie magazine. 1950

▶ Michèle Morgan taking off her *stockings* in the torrid, steamy heat of Mexico, recreated for *The Proud Ones* by Yves Allégret. 1953

◄ Joan Collins, *suspender belt* in battle order, using seduction to get what she wants. TV Film. 1960

▲ The unforgettable sequence where Cyd Charisse, a soviet agent, dances with a pair of *stockings,* a symbol of the decadent luxury of capitalist countries. In *Silk Stockings* by Rouben Mamoulian. 1957

▶ The only time that Grace Kelly showed the top of her *suspenders.* She was jumping with the photographer Philippe Halsman for his "Jumpology" series. 1959. © Photo: Philippe Halsman/Magnum Photos

The American woman in all her glory: the pioneer of the Wild West, rigged out and armed to the teeth, ready to fight off Indians or gangsters.

▲ Jane Russell in *The Outlaw* by Howard Hughes. 1940
◄ Janet Leigh in *Kid Rodeo* by Richard Carlson. 1965

According to legend, the only time
Marilyn Monroe ever wore knickers was
for Billy Wilder's *The Seven Year Itch*. 1955
And (left page), the risqué use made of
this legend by humorous cartoonists.
Here, Milo Manara. 1970s

Lingerie in Film 316 · 317

Like Jean Harlow, Marilyn always prided herself on wearing nothing under her clothes and on keeping her underwear in the freezer when the weather was roasting hot. Except when she wore *fishnet tights* for publicity shots or to play the role of a knicker-clad pioneering woman in *River of no Return* by Otto Preminger. 1954

Marilyn look-alikes, showing off their *knickers* as their legendary idol did, photographed in New York by Misha Erwitt. 1987
Following pages: Marilyn wearing *fishnet tights* or black *stockings*, posing, shortly before her death, for her friend, the photographer Milton Greene.

Following in Marilyn's footsteps, the well-endowed Jayne Mansfield in her angora underwear, highly impractical except for publicity shots. She also made the most of see-through fabrics, also for publicity. 1950s

Umpteenth remake of *The Blue Angel,* this time by Edward Dmytryk, with May Britt as Lola and Curd Jürgens as Professor Rath. 1959

Jean Desailly taking off Françoise Dorléac's stockings in François
Truffaut's *La peau douce.* 1963

Lee Remick in Tony Richardson's *Sanctuary.* 1960

A cult film gave its name to an item of lingerie and boosted sales of these
nightdresses to the tune of twenty-five million: *Baby Doll*, by Elia Kazan.
Carroll Baker, in a babydoll, not only sold her nightie by sucking her thumb,
she also caused the number of devotees of the act of fellatio to soar to 65% in
the subsequent *Kinsey Report*.

Jeanne Moreau was fond of wearing retro-style and kinky underwear, whether she was playing the part of a female spy in *Mata Hari, Agent H. 21*, the 1964 film by Jean-Louis Richard (left) or acting the role of a servant girl whose

master is fascinated by her ankle boots, which will be the death of him,
in *Diary of A Chambermaid* by Luis Buñuel, 1964 (right)

The devastating underwear worn by Brigitte Maier in *Sensations* by Lasse Braun. 1975

Judy Carné's simple underwear in *A Pair of Briefs*. 1962

An array of provocative *corsets*.
The sexy Second Empire lace-up corset in *La dame aux camélias* by
Mauro Bolognini. 1980

Prostitution (not forgetting the
allusive harp) by Maurice
Boutel. 1962

Dorothea Blanck swooning in her *corset* in *Lola* by Jacques Demy. 1960

One woman who had no compunction about showing off the *suspenders* stretched over her curvaceous thighs: Sophia Loren in *The Millionairess* by Anthony Asquith, 1960 (left) and off screen (right)

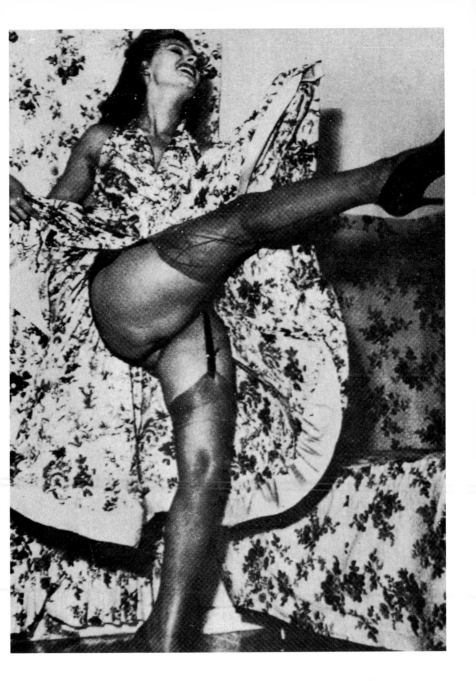

Sophia Loren's consummate striptease in *Yesterday, Today and Tomorrow* by Vittorio de Sica, 1963, in which she educates the young seminarist,

Marcello Mastroianni. He finally gives up the church in favour of
her – or her lingerie.

The striptease according to Fellini: Nadia Gray in *La dolce vita.* 1959

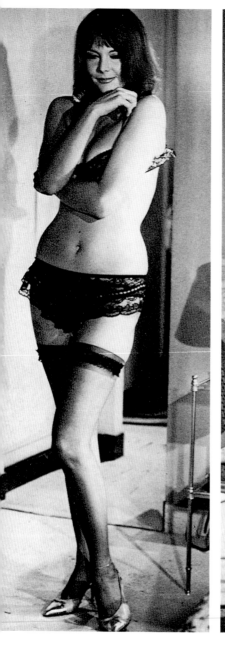

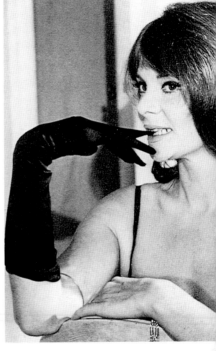

A classic example of the art of striptease on screen: Françoise Brion in *La Dénonciation* by Jacques Doniol-Valcroze. 1961

Following pages: Not forgetting the famous striptease by Raquel Welch, who removes her *knickers* in front of an audience including John Huston. 1960s

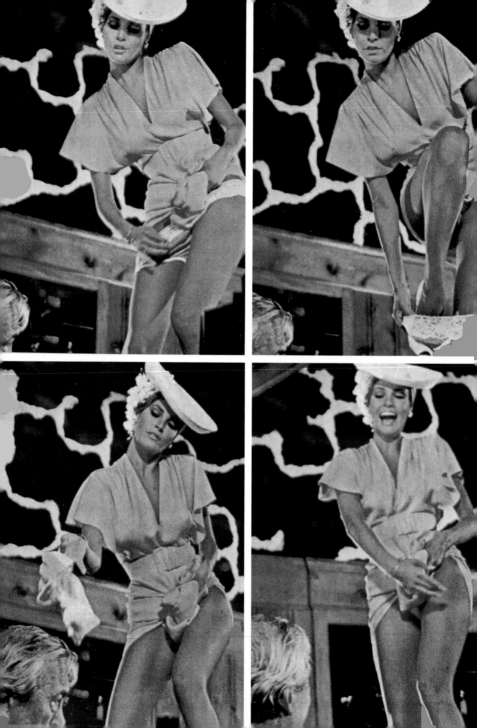

The curvaceous Elsa Martinelli, the star of *And to Die of Pleasure, The Threat* and *Misdeal,* stripping down to her black *stockings* for the last time, at the age of 46, in front of the photographer's camera

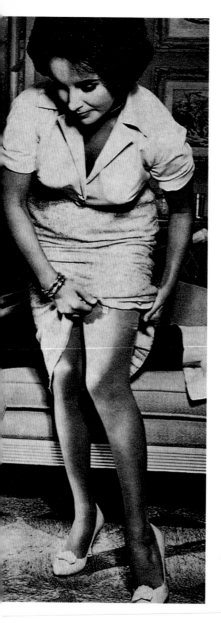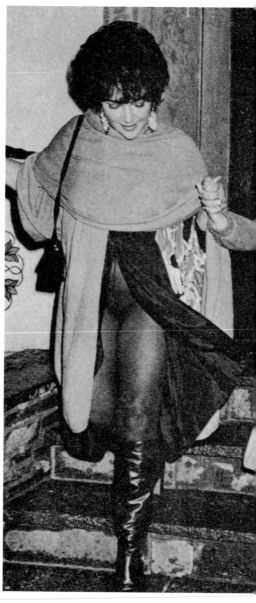

From *suspenders* to *tights:* Elizabeth Taylor's underwear on screen in *Cat on a Hot Tin Roof* by Richard Brooks, 1958, and off.

Classical, sexy black lace lingerie, worn by Ava Gardner.
Publicity shot. 1960s

◄ At the Cannes Festival in 1956, the already famous
Bardot showed her *briefs* to the press photographers.

▲ In *La Mariée était trop belle* by Pierre Gaspard-Huit of the same year,
Brigitte Bardot proudly wore a *waspie* made by the Star fashion house, which
has since given it pride of place in its private museum.

In *En Cas de Malheur* by Claude Autant-Lara, 1958, Bardot offers to pay her lawyer, Jean Gabin, in kind, and shows him a sample of the delights in store for him.

▲ A censored frame from the same sequence. B.B. was, it appears, *knickerless*.
▼ Bardot pays her debt.

Brigitte Bardot wearing a variety of underwear, as "Bonnie" (singing *Bonnie and Clyde* with Serge Gainsbourg on television) and as a nun.

▲ Ursula Andress changes her style of underwear from film to film. 1960s
◄ Bardot, still beautiful at the age of 40, photographed by Ghislain Dussart,
for the shooting of *Viva Maria* by Louis Malle. 1965

Prostitute by day and a
respectable woman by night,
Catherine Deneuve at the
brothel, in *Belle de Jour* by
Luis Buñuel. 1967

▼ A client, Francis Blanche, with Françoise Fabian and Maria Latour

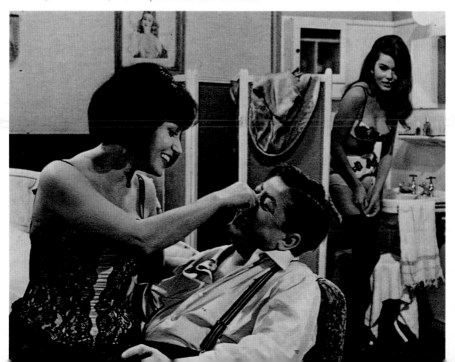

▲ "Women's legs are a pair of compasses which span the globe in every sense, ensuring harmony and balance," says the hero in François Truffaut's film *The Man Who Loved Women.* 1977
▼ In the same film, Geneviève Fontanel runs a women's lingerie shop.
▶ Voyeurism in *Onze Mille Verges* (Eleven Thousand Penises) by Lipman. 1970s

LES
onze mille
verges

TERDIT AUX MOINS DE 18 ANS

PLANFILM

▲ Stockings are the ultimate weapon of the mature woman, used to seduce
Dustin Hoffman, the teenager in Mike Nichols' film *The Graduate*. 1967
◄ "Don't look, sonny": *Paris Music-Hall* by Stany Cordier. 1956   **Lingerie in Film** 360 · 361

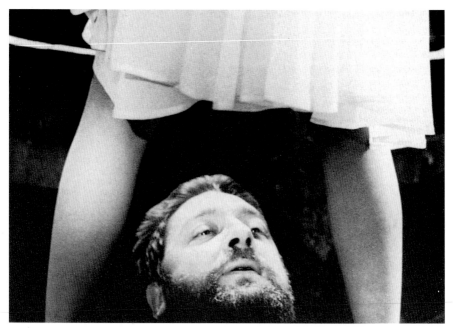

Voyeurism and lingerie on screen
▲ Richard Burton in *The Spy Who Came in from the Cold* by Martin Ritt. 1965
▼ The Peeping Tom in *Salo Or The 120 Days of Sodom* by Pier Paolo Pasolini. 1975

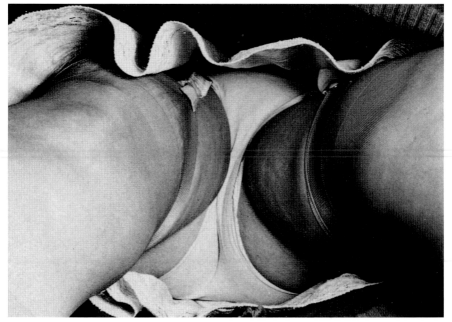

► Sequence from *Sex School*. 1960s
▲ The obliging secretary of Italian films. 1960s
▼ Surrealist voyeurism in *L'imitation du cinéma* by Marcel Mariën. 1960

Voyeurism and sexual harassment: Laura Antonelli, the unfortunate victim, is not as innocent as she seems. She knows how to make the most of her underwear in order to come out "on top". *Malicia*, a film by Salvatore Samperi. 1973

▲ Another sequence from *Malicia*, a complete education in sex – and cycling.
Here, Tina Aumont, watched avidly by her young comrade, learns how to get onto
a man's bike. This lascivious comedy was a huge success in Italy. 1973
◄ Another way of revealing your underwear to a young companion. Susan Player
in *L'Initiatrice* by Sergio Martino. 1970s

▲ *Swedish Specialities*, or the erotic appeal of retro-style lingerie, by Werner Hedman. 1975
▶ The kinky passions of Andréa Ferréol in *Servante et Maîtresse* by Bruno Gentillon. 1976

Following pages: In *The Key* by Tinto Brass, 1984, the elderly husband with a fetish for underwear takes advantage of his wife's accommodating sleep to photograph and rape her. This has become a cult film, heralding the rampant eroticism of the 1980s and the renewed popularity of the *suspender belt* as erotic accessory.

Imp. G. DARMON Paris

LA CLÉ

Interdit aux moins de 18 ans

V de C 10414

In *The Key*, by Tinto Brass, 1984, Stefania Sandrelli is the wife; she appears in a state of undress at the age of 40.

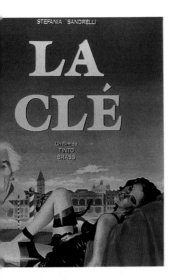

Another cult film made in 1960, *Peeping Tom* by Michael Powell has as its hero Karl-Heinz Böhm, a lonely and unbalanced young man and a film studio focus puller, who undresses his models before murdering them with a stiletto concealed in one of the legs of his camera. He catches their death agonies on film, then watches the end product at his leisure.

◄ Jane Birkin in a passionate embrace with Serge Gainsbourg. 1970s

◄ Michel Piccoli and his extremely lifelike inflatable doll,
with pubic hair and underwear

Lingerie worn by possessed women
▲ Sexual and hysterical madness sweeps through *L'intérieur d'un couvent* by Walerian Borowczyk, 1977, the Boccaccio of the 1970s ◄ Raquel Welch wearing *suspenders* straddling a phallic witch's broomstick in *Myra Breckinridge*, a film by Michael Sarne. 1970

A variety of sex symbols in Ken Russell's *Lisztomania*, 1975, or the excesses prompted by the film-maker's hatred for Wagner, who is unfairly shown as the father of Nazism.

The Rocky Horror Picture Show, a cult film by Jim Sharman, 1975, is a cross between
a horror film and a musical. A great favourite with transsexuals, it parodies a mad
doctor "Frankenstein", now a transsexual, who creates Rocky, the ideal man,
a transvestite in underwear.

▲ In the remake of *King-Kong* by John Guillermin, 1976, the monster, more in love than ever before with the heroine, manages to remove the *bra* of his idol, Jessica Lange.

▶ Another erotic remake (1936's *Flash Gordon*) renamed *Flesh Gordon*, with futuristic underwear, the heroine herself wearing strange metal *stockings*. 1970s

FLESH
GORDON

NOT TO BE CONFUSED WITH THE
ORIGINAL "FLASH GORDON"

COLOR

The lingerie worn by Romy Schneider in *Orage*. 1970s

The society prostitute: Monica Vitti in *Histoire d'aimer* by
Marcello Fondato. 1970

The sensible underwear worn by Jane Fonda is not always as innocent as it seems here.

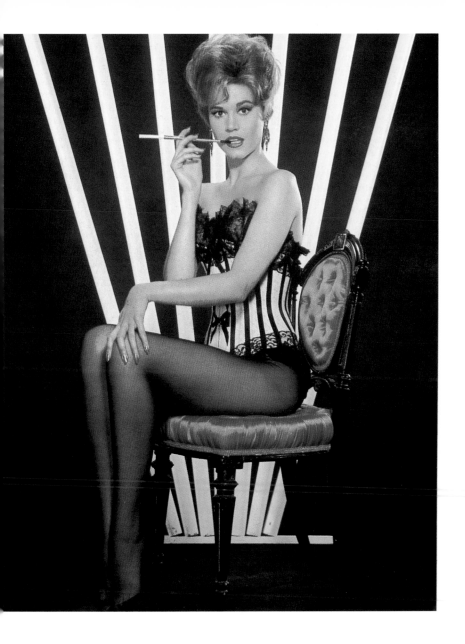

Particularly when she is posing for a publicity shot that plays on the fantasies
suggested by her cigarette-holder.

Although a tireless
campaigner for women's
rights, Jane Fonda also
took sex object parts.
Publicity photo accurately
representing the spirit of
the film *Barbarella* by
Roger Vadim. 1967

Claudia Cardinale dressed as a prostitute in *The Love Makers* by
Mauro Bolognini. 1961

Underwear worn by two Italian beauties: Laura Antonelli and Claudia Cardinale

The good old *waspie* is still a favourite. Pamela Green recalls Monica Vitti in *Histoire d'aimer* by Marcello Fondato. 1972

Once again, *Lola* by Jacques Demy. 1961. This time, Anouk Aimée is wearing a *corset*, her haughty yet ambiguous expression emphasised by her feather boa.

x

Lingerie in Film 392 · 393

Nastassja Kinski girds her loins in *Maria's Lovers.* 1984

AMERICAN COLLEGE

"NATIONAL LAMPOON"S ANIMAL HOUSE"

UN FILM UNIVERSAL DISTRIBUÉ PAR CINEMA INTERNATIONAL CORPORATION

TOUS DROITS DE REPRODUCTION, DE DIFFUSION ET DE VENTE STRICTEMENT RÉSERVÉS

American College by John Landis, 1978, or the underwear in the life of an American college in 1962

▲ Anna Karina transformed into a sailor of sorts by Jean-Luc Godard in *Une femme est une femme.* 1960
◄ Luis Buñuel, as usual, ignores taboos and freely indulges his fantasies in *The Phantom of Liberty,* 1974,
rigging out Anna-Maria Descott in leather, *suspenders* and a whip.

The sexy attire of the shell diver, Ursula Andress, created a stir and looked more like underwear than outerwear in the James Bond film *Doctor No* by Terence Young. 1962

"The army's a bitch." People get up to strange things in this Korean war field hospital. Here, "Hot Lips", the desirable major portrayed by Sally Kellerman, gets out of her helicopter, treating the troops to a generous glimpse of her *suspenders. M.A.S.H.* by Robert Altman. 1970

Beautiful Jessica Lange, having escaped from King-Kong, is now seducing Jack Nicholson on the kitchen table in *The Postman Always Rings Twice*. 1981

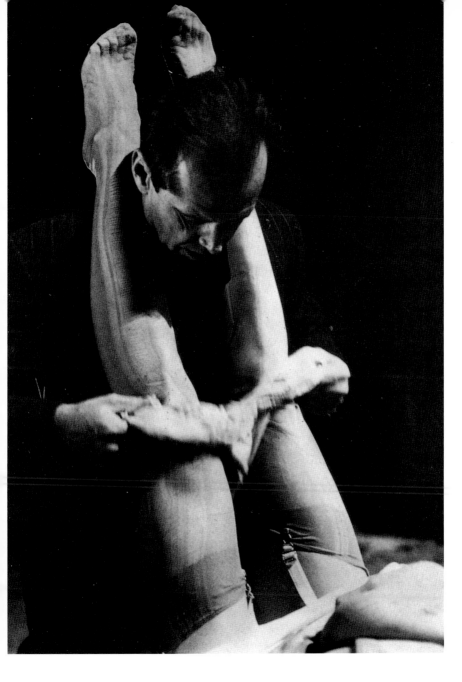

Jack Nicholson pulling off Jessica Lange's *knickers*. Censored sequence

9 1/2 SEMAINES

UN FILM DE **ADRIAN LYNE**

American-style striptease, more naïve than kinky, performed by the beautiful Kim Basinger who, for lack of other arguments, throws her *knickers* in Mickey Rourke's face. *9 1/2 Weeks* by Adrian Lyne. 1985

For his directing debut, Gian Maria Volonté pulled out all the stops. He chose the beautiful Di Lazzarro as his co-star, raping her next to the corpse of her husband whom he has just murdered. 1980s

The provocative *waspie* as worn by Fanny Ardant in *Paltoquet* by Michel Deville. 1986

In the train with *Madame Claude* by Just Jaeckin. 1980s

It took no less than six films and as many directors to recount the erotic escapades of *Emmanuelle*. In the first, made in 1973, Just Jaeckin shows us the heroine, Sylvia Kristel, acquiring an unsentimental education in Bangkok under her

husband's guidance. Before rejoining her accommodating husband in the East, Emmanuelle gives
herself to two passengers on the flight there, while pretending to be asleep (right). **Lingerie in Film 406 · 407**

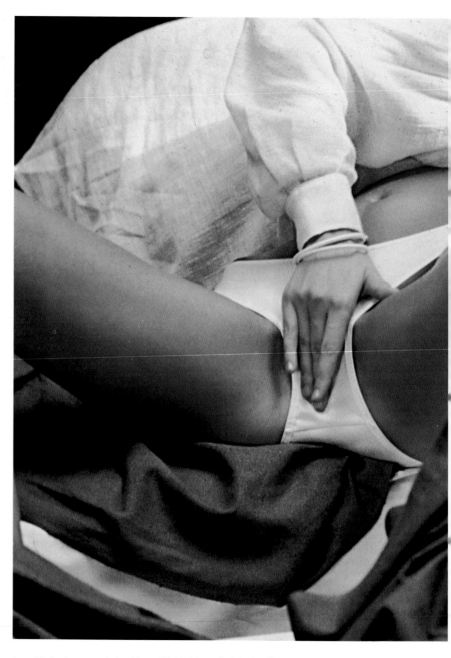

Anna-Maria, the young virgin with unsullied *knickers*, who is initiated by Emmanuelle and her husband in Just Jaeckin's *Emmanuelle.* 1973

The queen of French porn films in the 1970s and 1980s was Brigitte Lahaie, photographed here by Serge Jacques, between her two maids of honour.

▶ One of the sexiest women in the world, according to Americans, in leather and *hold-ups*, is Brigitte Nielsen, Rambo's former girlfriend. Photo Claude Sauer for *Paris-Match*. 1996

"Superwoman" (left) and "Supervixen" (championed by Russ Meyer, who favoured pneumatic breasts and belligerent thighs – right), set the trend for the intrepid lingerie worn by superwomen of the future.

Scandale

GAINES * CEINTURES * SOUTIEN-GORGE

Lingerie
in Advertising

*"I can resist everything
except temptation."*

OSCAR WILDE

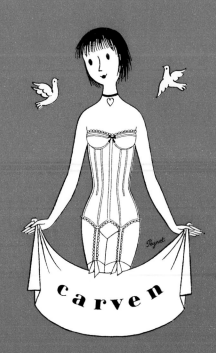

▶ Raymond Peynet: Carven *Half-cup Bra.* 1955
◀ Delmotte: Scandale *girdle,* or Eve and the serpent. 1947

IC A LA PERSÉPHONE

175332

CORSETS
DE PARIS

LE CORSET
SANS GÊNE

U. V.

c'est l'élegance
c'est la qualité
c'est la souplesse
c'est la durée
c'est la grâce
c'est la santé
c'est le bien être

C'EST LE CORSET PARFAIT

IMP.PICHOT 54 Rue de Clichy PARIS

▲ In 1893, actress Réjane was performing to packed houses in the play
by Victorien Sardou, *Madame Sans-Gêne*. A *corset* of the same name
capitalised on the success of this artiste, seen here in a poster by
Gallicelo. Circa 1910

◄ Anonymous: A La Perséphone. 1889. First use of a mirror in an
advertisement, here, to show the back of the *corset*.

MADAME DOWDING,

8 & 10, CHARING CROSS ROAD (Opposite the National Gallery, Trafalgar Square),

Ladies' Tailor, Corsetiere, and Court Dressmaker.

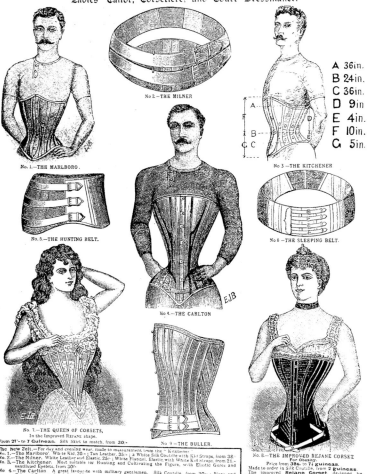

No 2.—THE MILNER

No. 1.—THE MARLBORO.

No 3.—THE KITCHENER

A 36in.
B 24in.
C 36in.
D 9in
E 4in
F 10in.
G 5in.

NO. 5.—THE HUNTING BELT.

No 6.—THE SLEEPING BELT.

No 4.—THE CARLTON

No. 7.—THE QUEEN OF CORSETS,
In the Improved REJANE shape.
From 2¹'- to 7 Guineas. Silk Skirt to match, from 30.-

No 9.—THE BULLER.

No 8.—THE IMPROVED REJANE CORSET
For Obesity.
Price from 38s. to 7½ guineas.
Made to order in Silk Coutille, from 2 guineas.
The improved Rejane Corset, designed by
Madame Dowding, is declared by several of the West
End doctors to be the most perfect of any "anatomi-
cal" Corset yet invented, and supplies a long felt
requirement to those habitually inclined to "embon-
point." This new Corset has been tried with marvel-
lous results by ladies inclined to obesity.

The New Belt.—For day and evening wear, made to measurement from the "Kitchener."
No. 1.—The Marlboro'. White Kid, 30.-; Tan Leather, 35.-; a White Silk Coutille with Kid Straps, from 38.-
No. 2.—The Milner. White Leather and Elastic, 25.-; White Flannel, Elastic with White Kid straps, from 21.-
No. 3.—The Kitchener. Most suitable for Hunting and Cultivating the Figure, with Elastic Gores and
     ventilated Eyelets, from 30/-
No 4.—The Carlton. A great favourite with military gentlemen. Silk Coutille, from 30/-; Black and
     Coloured Sateens, lined, from 50.-
No. 5.—The Hunting Belt. Tan Leather, 30/-; Coutille, with Leather Bands, from 30.-
No. 6.—The Sleeping Belt. White Flannel with Elastic Gores and perforated Eyelets. The first Belt for
     Cultivating the Figure.
No. 9.—The Buller. A most comfortable shape for day or evening wear, made in all materials, from 35/- to
     6 guineas. Most popular Belt for gentlemen inclined to obesity.
     All these Belts are absolutely Hygienic, and can only be procured from Madame DOWDING, the Sole Inventor and Designer
No orders can be executed under seven days' notice. The demand for these Corsets is daily increasing, and is, indeed, a great advertisement to the Inventor.
MADAME DOWDING begs to thank the numerous West End Tailors for their kind recommendations. All Communications STRICTLY PRIVATE in Belt Dept.

▲ English patent for *corsets* for women and men. 1899
▶ *Underskirt* for a crinoline. 1862
◀ American *corset*. 1898. Anonymous: Le Sanita. 1890. Underwear becomes
synonymous with good health.

N.D. *corsets.* 1906. The main selling point of these corsets was that they were quick and easy to remove, a very practical consideration for La Belle Otéro, a celebrated Belle Epoque *demi-mondaine* and actress depicted here, who had worked her way through countless lovers.

HYGIÈNE, ÉLÉGANCE, SOUPLESSE

CORSET

LE FURET

BREVETÉ S.G.D.G.

maintient mais ne comprime pas

Donne la Souplesse de l'Orientale avec la grâce Française

Poster by Léonetto Capiello (a contemporary of Toulouse-Lautrec)
for the Le Furet *corset*. 1901. Ferrets *(furets)* are proverbially slender.

Lingerie in Advertising 420 · 421

LE VÉRITABLE CORSET
PERSÉPHONE
REND PLUS SVELTES LES PLUS SVELTES PARISIENNES

CES ELÉGANTS CORSETS DE PARIS SONT EN VENTE DANS UN DES PREMIERS MAGASINS DE SPÉCIALITÉ POUR CORSETS · GÉNERALEMENT
LE PREMIER · DE PRESQUE CHAQUE VILLE, ET DANS LES MAISONS SPECIALES DU CORSET PERSÉPHONE CI·APRES ·

PARIS : 187, RUE SAINT·HONORE	CORSET PERSÉPHONE **910**, BREVETÉ S G D G	ROUEN : 21, RUE DE LA RÉPUBLIQUE
LE HAVRE : 75, RUE DE PARIS	EN BATISTE DAMASSÉE RICHE .... 125 fr	NANTES : 24, RUE DU CALVAIRE
LILLE : 21, BOULEVARD CARNOT	EN BATISTE SOIE UNIE .... 70 fr	MARSEILLE : 51, RUE SAINT·FERRÉOL
TOULON : 3, RUE EMILE ZOLA	EN COUTIL BLANC, FLEURETTES SOIE .... 45 fr	ST·ETIENNE : 18, RUE DE LA RÉPUBLIQUE
TOURS : 43, RUE NATIONALE	EN BATISTE FAÇONNÉE BLANCHE .... 37 fr	
	EN TRES JOLI COUTIL PEKINE, TOUTES NUANCES ... 29 fr	

Maximilian Fischer: The Perséphone *corset*. 1912. Front and rear views of the *corset* which made "svelte Parisiennes even slimmer".

THE "SPECIALITÉ CORSET"

IS A DREAM OF COMFORT.

The beautiful odalisque of the 1900s, languidly resting in the "comfort" of her *corset*.

Corsets BALEININE INCASSABLES

Bté S.G.D.G.

Souplesse Elégance Solidité

Alfred Chonbrac. Circa 1900. The leading lights of the French Belle Epoque give their vote of confidence to the sturdy Baleinine *corset,* reinforced by whalebone. From left to right and from the most curvaceous to the thinnest: Jeanne Bloch, Polaire, Emilienne d'Alençon, Cléo de Mérodes, Eve Lavallière

The supposedly unbreakable Baleinine *corset* with its precious cargo. It was also healthy, sophisticated and, most importantly, strong. Circa 1900

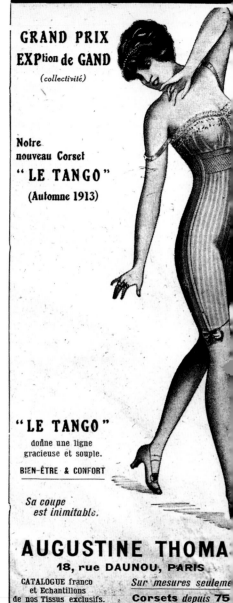

Women could dance in Le Tango by Augustine Thomas. 1913

AS MONDIA
FABRICATION FRANÇAISE
MARQUE DÉPOSÉE

Augustine Thomas, or the comforts of home. Circa 1900

Mondia *stockings* were apparently lighter than air.
Circa 1900

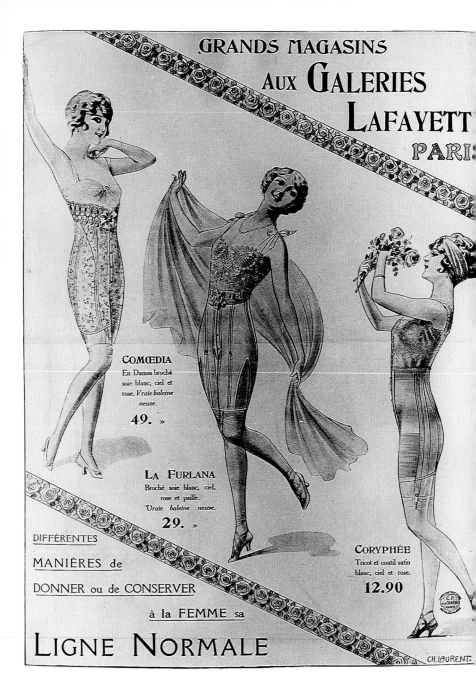

The Galeries Lafayette in Paris guaranteed that the woman of the 1900s would retain her natural shape.

LIBRON & C.ie

La Mode

Select-Corset
J.B.P.

PARIS

19·Rue Louis le Grand

▲ The Libron *corset.* 1912

◄ Although somewhat complicated and unwieldy, this American patent design was effective in holding up the *stockings* and preventing the *corset* from riding up.

"No Clasps to Grip the Hose and Rip"

DICKINS
& JONES

THE "SPECIALITÉ" Reg.d STRAIGHT FRONTED CORSET

Type 8.—THE STRAIGHT-FRONTED TYPE OF THE "SPECIALITE CORSET" (as illustration) is very popular, being modelled on the lines of the best French Corsets and equal in cut and quality to those

▲ Dickins & Jones in competition with France. 1910

In the 1920s, under the influence of French designer Poiret, the *corset* became the Extra Souple girdle.

Théo Matykos: Wefka. 1919. Cupid makes a slightly risqué gesture with his arrow to demonstrate the elasticity of these *garters*.

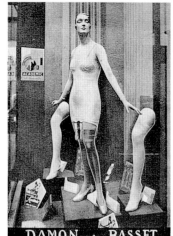

► Damon & Basset showcase at the Exposition Coloniale, Paris. 1931

From the French Belle Epoque to the Roaring Twenties:
▲ German *bust-improver*. Circa 1900
► Cover of the Neyret lingerie catalogue. 1925. The loose-fitting *slip* replaces the restrictive *corset*.

Le Furet is still at large. Poster by Roger Pérot. 1933

Von Allmen: The she-cat, a female symbol, wearing a pink *corset* by Viso. 1920s

behaglich
elegant
waschbar
Enkalon
Strümpfe Wäsche Stoffe
geprüfte Qualität

Herbert Leupin for Enkalon. 1960. Forty years later, the formula has not changed: the she-cat has made a comeback, wearing the same ribbon around her neck as her grandmother to emphasise the femininity of the product.

Arwa, seamed *stockings* that can weather any storm. 1935

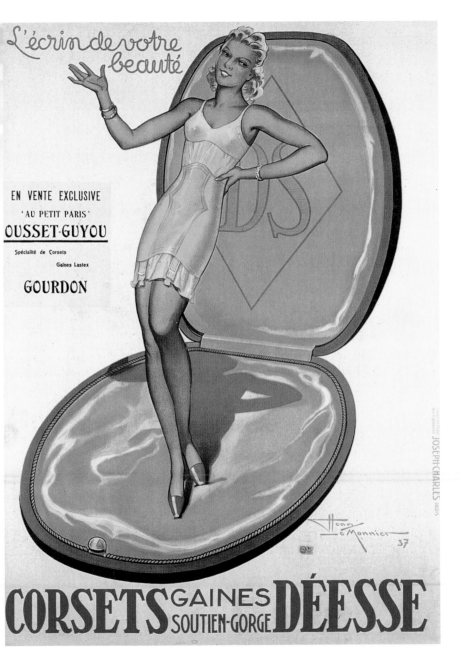

"The perfect setting for your beauty", as seen by Henri Le Monnier,
clearly inspired by his old friend Botticelli. 1937

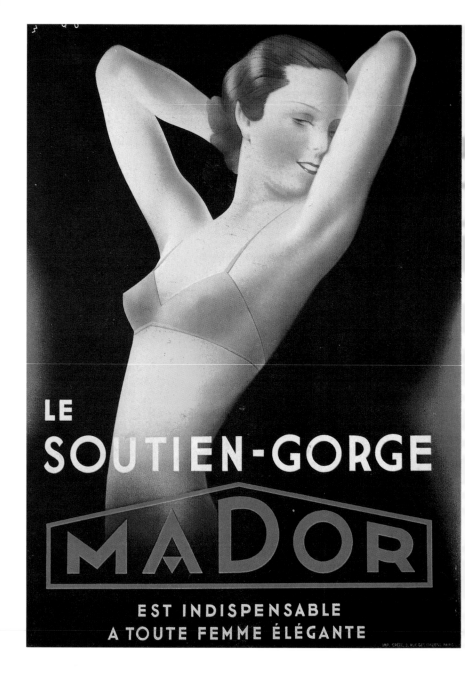

André Wilquin: The Mador *bra* is a must for comfort with sex-appeal. Circa 1930

PHOTO LAURE ALBIN GUILLOT

Le soutien gorge

Cibil

BREVETÉ S. G. D. G.

tient et maintient
sans épaulettes

The Cibil strapless *bra*, photographed by Laure Albin-Guillot in the 1930s,
brings back memories of the tea-strainer *bra* first patented in England.

Emeric Feher: Living up to its name, Scandale had courageously decided to focus on eroticism before the war. In 1939, patriotism entered the equation and Eve's serpent became the three-coloured flag of France.

Culotte "Vélo-Ski"

MADOR
32 et 34, RUE DES JEUNEURS
PARIS

EST INDISPENSABLE AUX SPORTIVES ÉLÉGANTES

André Wilquin: Vélo-Ski *panties*. In 1939, women became more interested in sports, taking up cycling and skiing. An obliging gust of wind shows that they have swapped their cumbersome knickers for tight-fitting elasticised briefs.

BY REDFERN

©1937 WBCO

▲ Warner used skiing, a luxury sport at the time, to promote its elasticised range of lingerie. 1937

▶ Le Gant, made of "youthlastic", so stretchy it fitted like a glove, was perfect for women at the wheel. 1935

Le Gant

en "YOUTHLASTIC"
qui s'étire en tous sens

LE GANT
Warner's
s'étire en tous sens.
C'est l'accomplisse-
ment d'un rêve
pour les femmes
du monde
entier.

... GANT, comme une seconde peau, se
... te à tous les mouvements du corps.

... GANT, qu'on ne sent pas est indis-
... sable à toutes celles qui ne peuvent
... porter la moindre gêne.

... GANT ne se roule pas, évite les bour-
... s. C'est l'article idéal pour toutes les
... ttes, le voyage, les sports.

... GANT existe pour chaque silhouette.
... nde ou petite, forte au mince, il y a un
... èle Le Gant pour toute femme soucieuse
... a ligne.

... GANT, tissé Lastex, est breveté

Ceintures à partir de . . 175 frs.
Corselettes à partir de. 275 frs.
Soutiens gorge à partir de 45 frs.

Renseignements et vente en gros :
Warner'-Aiglon
14, Boulevard Poissonnière - Paris

EN VENTE CHEZ :
- 80, Rue Saint-Lazare - 7, Boulevard Haussmann
- Rue Saint-Honoré, dans les grands magasins et dans
... maisons de corsets du monde entier.

▲ Pastel colours for pre-war underwear. Kestos. 1939
◄ Freedom is the key note of this advertisement, published in the magazine *Corsets and Brassieres*, United States. 1937
► Kestos: The Three Graces are now all platinum blondes like Jean Harlow. 1937

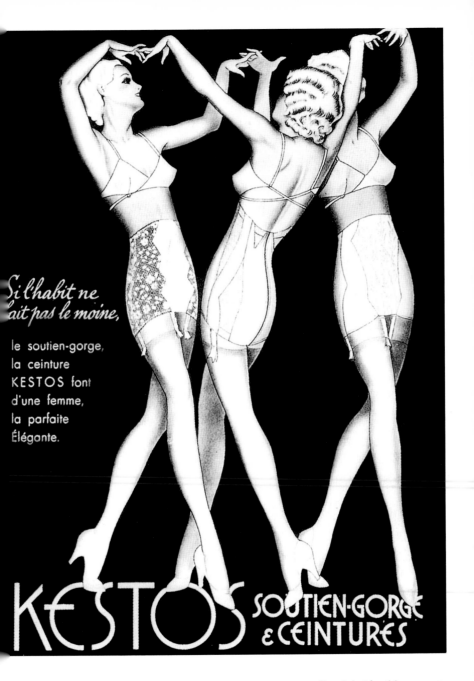

Si l'habit ne
ait pas le moine,

le soutien-gorge,
la ceinture
KESTOS font
d'une femme,
la parfaite
Élégante.

KESTOS SOUTIEN-GORGE
& CEINTURES

Ein Wunder

die bedri
- Nadel

zum Maschenheben

▲ Having taken refuge in the United States during the war, Salvador Dali played his part in the launch of nylon *stockings* in 1944. On this occasion, Bryan *stockings*.

◄ During this period, poverty reigned on the continent. It was no longer possible to buy new *stockings*, only tools to darn old ones. 1940

Poster for the Moulin Rouge, 1945: *stockings* were back in the limelight, especially nylon *stockings*, which had been brought from America by GIs and were an overnight sensation.

dorland

Berlin
hat Chic!
Und hier der Trick:

tilly

Strümpfe

100% Perlon

The Paris-Berlin connection: Germany and France made their peace and in 1947 the artist Hib had the inspired idea of balancing the toe of his dancer, symbolising Paris, on the muzzle of a bear, the emblem of Berlin. This marked the beginning of a common market for lingerie.

These girls look like wax models because the censors forbade them to look too lifelike: they had to stay completely still and expressionless.

PHOTO DEVAL

Barbara

CECILE

Aubade. 1947 ▲ Barbara. 1947

More wax models but this time in Technicolor. If they had moved, they might have been mistaken for strippers. Aubade designs. 1950s

► The plumage of the
pretty little Colibri. 1951
►► Aubade, "the *girdle*
of the century". 1954

GAINE Colibri
Paris

ubade

LA GAINE DU SIÈCLE

Lou introduced "the cleverest *bra*", so named probably because it was strapless. The bathing beauty changing on the beach is shielded from sight by a towel held by her inquisitive companion. The advent of a man in this feminine world was extremely daring for the time. 1950s

Donald Brun, circa 1950, came up with a mythological *bra*:
Niké, the Greek goddess of Victory

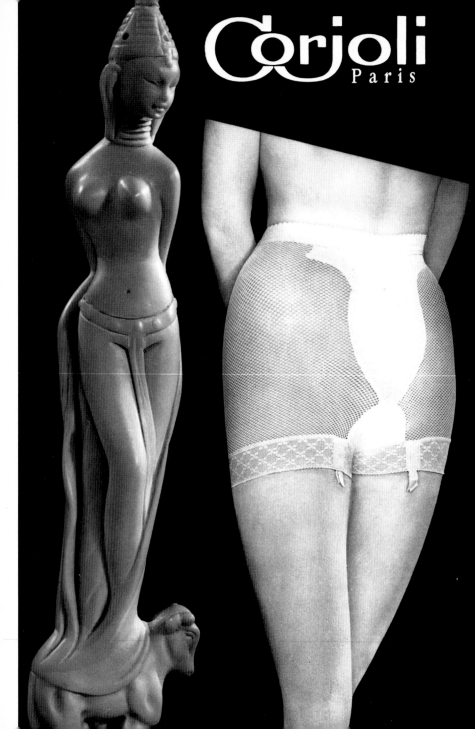

Corjoli
Paris

Corjoli
Paris

le "JUPANT"
M. déposé

Two "historical" inventions from Corjoli, 1950s:
▲ The "Jupant", a *panty girdle* and short *slip* combined.
◄ The fishnet-effect *Cage à mouches,* a restrictive *panty girdle*
which continued to restrict for many years.

SOUTIEN-GORGE

ROSY

PLAISIR DES YEUX

PUBLICIS

Philippe Foré, *bra* from Rosy, "a treat for the eyes". 1954

▲ Publicity photos: the Barbara range from the 1950s
▶ Soli-laine. Lingerie deserves to be washed with care, ideally, it seems,
by your black maid. 1954

LUXE 41

SPLENDOR N° 3

Barbara

Jaques Snépic

SOLI laine

une dose **SOLI-***laine* *lave tout ça !*

René Gruau made his mark on lingerie advertising in the 1950s. Here, a woman, not a man, reads the paper, allowing the spectator to focus on her *stockings* in all safety.

POUR PAQUES OFFREZ

BAS ET LINGERIE

J.-L. Lavaux for Vitos. Circa 1950. In this advertisement, too,
the woman is effaced in favour of her underwear.

Raymond Savignac: Star-billing for Perlon *stockings* from Opal. 1955

▼ The embarrassed sandwich man, by Hervé Morvan, appears to be wearing the women's underwear he is promoting. Circa 1950

BAS BOMO
gaiuent tellement mieux la jambe

▲ Here, the sandwich "man" is a shapely pin-up wearing the Bomo *stockings* she is advertising. Circa 1950

Lesage for Scandale. Circa 1950. As in Walt Disney's animated cartoon film, enchanting little birds are weaving stockings for Cinderella.

Anonymous for Bel *stockings*. 1951. Yet more birds, but these are doves,
symbols of gentleness, femininity and Venus.

The wax models used by prudish advertisers have now earned the right to move and there is no stopping them. They have tasted freedom and are keen for more. They go by helicopter with Stemm, left, or by jet, with Le Bourget stockings, right. 1950s

Transparents comme l'air!

BAS

le bourget

FABRIQUÉS Á
FRESNOY-LE-GRAND
(AISNE) • DANS LES USINES LES PLUS MODERNES D'EUROPE •

elle maintient !

L es sports, la voiture, les affaires, imposent aux femmes des fatigues qu'ignoraient leurs grand' mères. La gaine SCANDALE sait compenser les faiblesses du corps féminin et cependant lui laisser toute sa souplesse et son aisance.

B eauté et santé sont l'œuvre de la gaine SCANDALE. *Son tulle garanti* au tissage spécialement étudié, fait que souple et ferme tout à la fois elle moule sans causer aucune gêne. Et la coquetterie n'y perd pas ses droits. La ligne actuelle de la mode ne tolérant aucune imperfection, la gaine SCANDALE invisible et toujours présente, modèlera votre corps aux mesures exactes qu'imposent nos couturiers.

SCANDALE

PARIS : 26, Rue Vignon ; 73, Faubourg Saint-Honoré ; 36 bis, Avenue de l'Opéra ; 17, Boulevard Raspail
LYON : 7, Rue de la République. — MARSEILLE : 11, Rue de la Darse. — NICE : 1, Rue du Maréchal Pétain
BRUXELLES : 101, Rue de Namur. — LONDRES : 81, Great Portland Street. — TURIN : 237, Corso Vitto
Emanuele II. — BEYROUTH, Souk Tawile. CHEZ LES BONNES CORSETIERES ET DANS LES GRANDS MAGAS

TULLE GARANTI
LA GAINE EN

Création Yves Alexan
Publ. M. Noirclere

NUE OU NON non bien sûr, mais presque oui

combinu
pantynu
de
Barbara

Sté des MATIÈRES PLASTIQUES
M. R. B.
7, Boulevard Pasteur, 7
93 - LA COURNEUVE
TÉLÉPH. 833-55-99

Découvrir COMBINU de Barbara.
c'est parfaire votre ligne
en ayant l'impression d'être presque nue.
C'est être silhouettée sans aucune gêne.
C'est concilier l'inconciliable
avec la nouvelle texture extra-fine de Barbara.
Elle vous offre huit façons d'être nue ou non,
en uni, en florisé, en blanc, en chair.

16, faubourg saint-denis - Paris 10° - téléphone 824.53.99

▲ With Barbara, woman were almost naked. 1960s
◄ With Scandale, they could run and jump. Late 1950s

LOU

LA PLUS BELLE PARURE DU MONDE

This curvaceous, black-skinned blonde, created by the talented Pierre Brenot, has it all. 1957. Unfortunately, the bashful Lou label, like a *G-string*, has intervened.

LINGERIE, BAS

Ciel de France

Société Suménoise - Sumène - Gard

This advertisement for Ciel de France, also by Pierre Brenot, is more daring.
1959. This is indeed a celestial beauty. The knee resting on a rumpled bed
sheet leaves everything to the imagination.

Rosy la rose inspires the sincerest form of flattery
▲ Corjoli. 1965
▶▶ Triumph. 1968
Referring to this floral motif, the publicist Séguéla remarked: "Jean Feldman, the Zeus of communications, whispered in my ear: 'Ideas are like spermatozoids, there are millions of them, but only one will clear all the obstacles and procreate.'"

◄ Jean Feldman: Rosy, the woman with the rose. 1962. This poster, plastered over every wall in Paris, was the making of the agency. For the first time, there was no sign of the product. Woman had become the product itself, a slave to industry, what Klossowski called "living currency". The nude, like a mutilated statue, becomes an abstract fantasy, while the rose focuses attention on the label. The photographer used was the illustrious Jeanloup Sieff. The nude, English fashion model Helen April, did not want to be recognised, so they simply cropped her head.

SHEER COLOUR TIGHTS AND STOCKINGS

9 OUT OF 10 CATS PREFER THEM

'Feel the difference' **PP** PRETTY POLLY

The English label, Pretty Polly, opted for a more humorous approach. 1960s. This advertisement plays on the slang meaning of "cat" ("man"). When the cat rubs up against her, it erects its tail, while the model stands with legs apart.

Jacques Chardoz for Scandale, 1963, with a reminder that underwear
is closely associated with voyeurism.

collant Chesterfield voile fin

SPÉCIAL

extensible

Ceinture Elastomère Lycra®
Pointe et talon
renforcés, 15 D.
Fibre polyamide.

6,95 F

1
35
36

In the 1960s, *tights* superseded *suspender belts,* which then came to seem old-fashioned.

▲ Aslan for Chesterfield, 1975, or the argument for transparent fabrics.

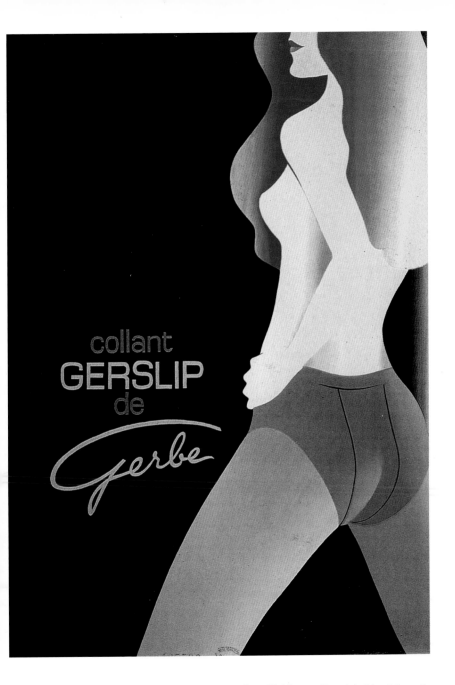

▲ Alain Gauthier for Gerbe, 1967, or the benefit of all-in-one *tights* and *briefs.*   **Lingerie in Advertising 476 · 477**

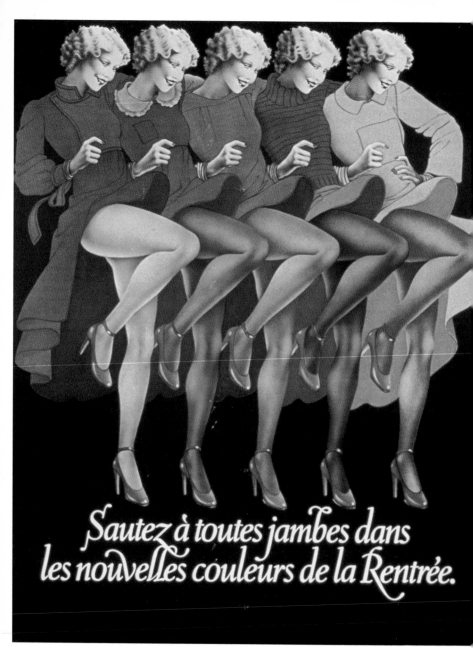

Sautez à toutes jambes dans
les nouvelles couleurs de la Rentrée.

▲ "Everyone in *tights*", like showgirls, was the rallying cry from Exciting in 1965. But where was the "excitement"?
▶ Pretty Polly, stretch Lycra *tights*. 1972. The English revealed the practical side to their nature and their fine
technical expertise, with their so-called "sack of potatoes" – but there was no eroticism in it.

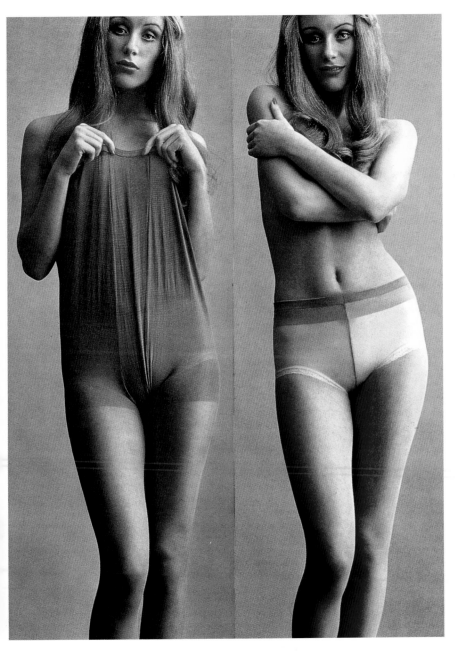

Following pages: In 1967, Arthur Penn's film *Bonnie and Clyde* was a great hit. Jean Feldman immediately capitalised on this, depicting his "Bonnies" in Ergé *hold-ups,* extremely practical for – well – hold-ups.

SPECIAL

SCHWEPPES GINGER ALE

64
en
LA COULEUR

Ci-dessus. L'ensemble poids plume, gaine en tulle Lycra (39,50 F env.) et soutien-gorge en Nylon et tulle Lycra (21,50 F env.), blancs imprimés de fleurs. Triumph. A gauche. Rouge et gai, un panty en Nylon et Lycra Spandex (77 F env.) et son soutien-gorge en Nylon, Lycra Spandex et dentelle de Nylon (49 F env.). Warner. Bas rayés en laine et Nylon mousse Helanca de Maix. Au milieu et ci-dessous, la nouvelle Petite Scandale imprimée rose ou bleu ciel. Lycra et Helanca (34,50 F env.). Soutien-gorge pour grand décolleté. Scandale.

Fleuries, rayées, unies, à petits carreaux jeunes, gaies, colorées, voici les nouvelles coordonnées 64

▲ The advertising industry is never stuck for an idea. Here, Triumph, Warner and Scandale designs are shown alongside cigar bands or beer labels. Photos by Helmut Newton. 1970
▶ Dim. 1971. Narcissism of the model, voyeurism of the spectator

Topin, for Triumph. 1970. A reference to hippie fashions

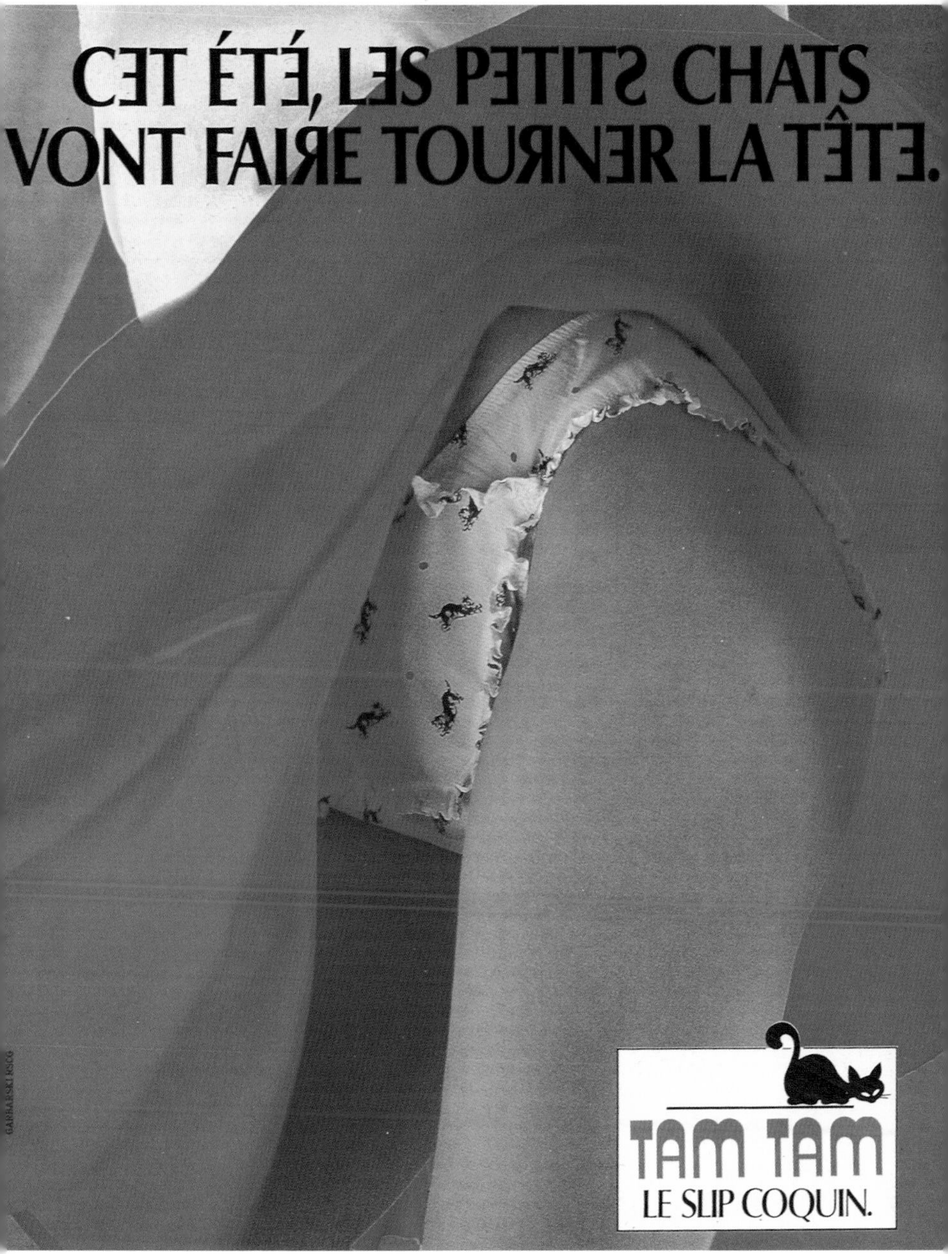

CET ÉTÉ, LES PETITS CHATS
VONT FAIRE TOURNER LA TÊTE.

TAM TAM
LE SLIP COQUIN.

Tam Tam added a touch of colour with its cheeky *briefs*,
soon to travel the world. 1970s

Tam Tam took their *briefs* on safari to update taboos in Arab countries (left page) and in Africa (right page).

La petite culotte qui rajeunit les tabous.

Avant la beauté était une. Cri d'horreur des missionnaires : « tabou, tabou, adorons la culotte ». Dessus, dessous la culotte est partout. Plantation : nuit tropique. Moto ville : rêve sage. Rajeunissons les tabous.

TAM TAM de Bambou :
la culotte passe-partout

In the 1980s, Chantal Thomass drew her inspiration from French Belle Epoque embroidery to enhance the erotic appeal of *tights*.

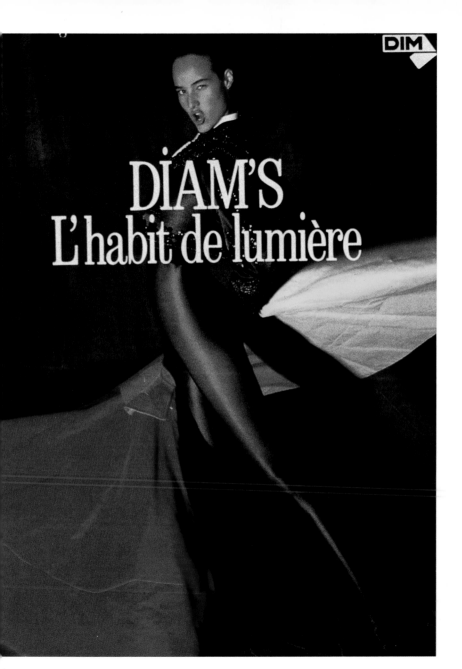

DIAM'S
L'habit de lumière

Dim went to the bullring for its inspiration because, after all, the toreador's
outfit *(l'habit de lumières)* includes a pair of *tights*.

Lou amused its customers with puns. After LOUtrance (outrageousness), LOUragan (hurricane), there was NewLOU – in homage probably to Christian Dior's New Look – and LOUtremer (overseas), probably a reference to the former colonies: spotlessly white underwear displayed against

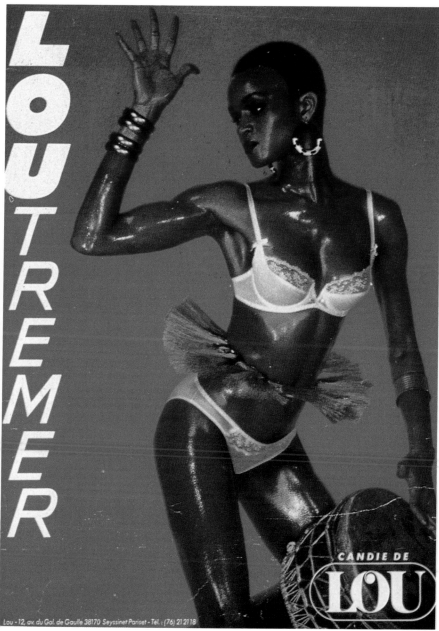

the dusky, oiled skin of a model following in
the footsteps of Josephine Baker.

In the 1980s, men started to make a timid appearance in women's advertising, as if to remind the world that lingerie was ultimately aimed at men.

▲ The man is nothing but a shadow for Dior. 1984

▲ The man's shoes insinuate themselves into this advertisement for Barbara. 1985
Following pages: "Aubade for a man" introduced colour and created a scandal. The man no longer hesitates to place his dominant hand on his consenting victim. 1986

Aubade pour un homme.

Above and following pages: The current trend for vinyl "S&M" underwear has led to a thriving mail-order
business used by people keen to organise select orgies in the privacy of their own homes. Here, various eye-

catching designs from P. Catanzaro's 1997–1998 catalogue, including bras that leave the breasts bare, zipped briefs and figure-hugging body sheaths, photographed by Christophe Mourthé, the king of sadomasochism.

La fibre qui, en toute circonstance, réagit en souplesse.

Toujours à la mode avec Dorlastan. La fibre de haute performance qui confère à la mode une fonction d'élasticité élevée et de pouvoir permanent de retour à la forme initiale. Dorlastan est, dans la maille, le bon génie qui, même en cas de sollicitations élevées, assure la conservation de la forme.

La maxi élasticité !

Contactez-nous pour recevoir notre documentation.

Bayer S.A., Division Fibre,
49 – 51, Quai de Dion Bouton,
F-92815 Puteaux Cedex,
Téléphone (1) 49.06.53.12

Dorlastan
Bayer Elastan
fantastic elastic

Bayer

y extension, women's underwear is also used to sell all kinds of luxury items.
Vuitton obviously felt that the lucky owner of this luggage needed to wear black *stockings*.
A mischievous parakeet demonstrates that Bayer's elastic fibre is a must for showing off a woman's curves to their
est advantage.

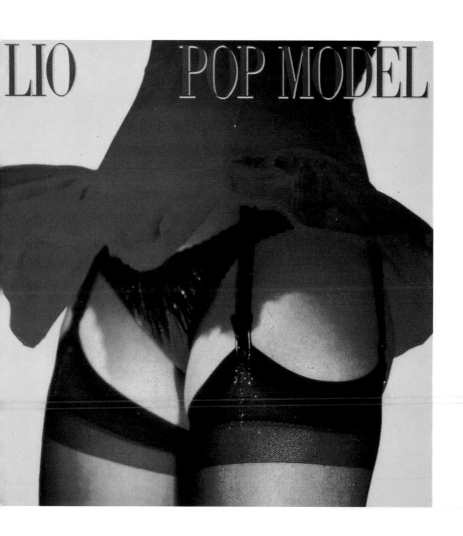

LIO   POP MODEL

The pop singer, Lio, is more than happy to show her
nickers to sell her record. 1995
Jean-Paul Gaultier uses a retro-style *corset* to sell his
perfume. 1997

Lingerie
and Eroticism

*"Women make men
act like fools."*

SALVADOR DALI

◄ Jean Dulac: *The Dirty Old Man.* Drawing for *Les Dessous d'un demi-siècle.* 1956
◄ *Her Master's Hand.* Photo by Serge Jacques for *Paris-Hollywood.* 1950s

◄ *Le Nu Esthétique,*
1903, reinvented
the first under-
garments worn by
Eve, a leafy branch
or two.

The late 19th century had already plumbed the depths of eroticism and photographic hypocrisy. Under the pretext of providing models for professional artists, Emile Bayard published *Le Nu Esthétique,* a magazine of nude "academic studies", supported by the Institute of France and the highly respected painter and sculptor J.-L. Gérome.

◄ The French Academy, in its turn, invented the first artistic *briefs*, a metal "shell". *Le Nu Esthétique.* 1903

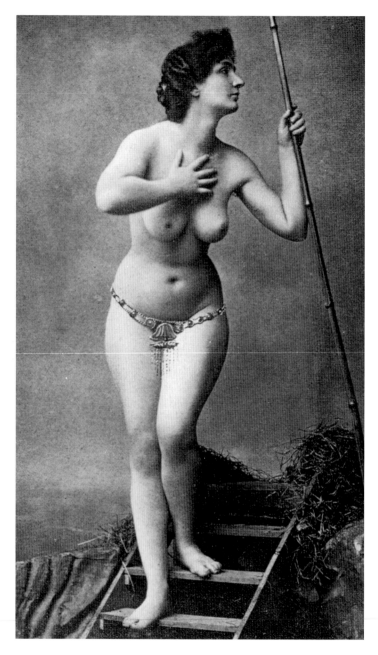

L'Etude Académique was another precursor of *Playboy*. 1909. The "shell" became a piece of Art Nouveau jewellery as tastes grew more sophisticated.

French Belle Epoque jewellers designed a dazzling array of bejewelled *bras, garters* studded with precious
stones, and a new generation of *knickers* and *chastity belts* made of precious metals and gems. *Demi-mondaines*

were given them as gifts by their nabobs and Reutlinger took photographs of these women decked out in all their finery in his studio.

The newly-invented bicycle was an excuse for wearing striped *stockings* and contriving more or less likely poses. 1900
Following pages: Toulouse-Lautrec's girlfriends and models liked to wear black stockings, which were also the
cheapest. From left to right: Grille d'égout (Sewage-cover), La Goulue (Big mouth/greedy) and Rayon d'or

Goldbeam). These French Can-Can dancers were often fined
the Moulin Rouge for high-kicking *knickerless.*

Erotic postcards of nudes, with or without underwear, were a thriving industry in the 1900s, when (elsewhere) women were cloaked from head to toe and seemed inaccessible.

1900 – The Belle Epoche

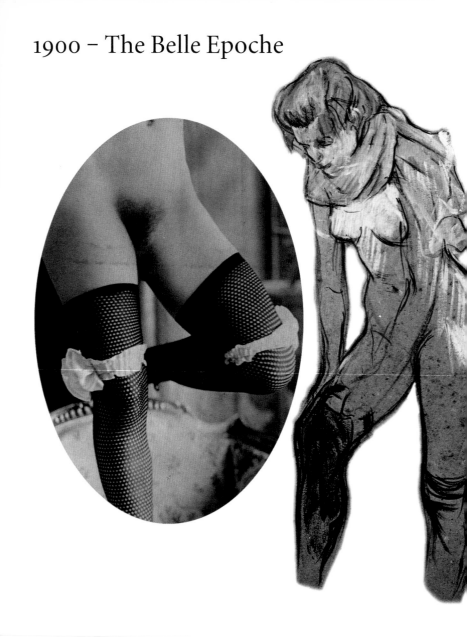

▲ Anonymous: *The Pretty Girl*. 1895
◄ Toulouse-Lautrec: *Woman Putting on her Stockings*. 1894

▲ Anonymous: *The Stockings.* 1896
◄ One of Toulouse-Lautrec's models. 1894

Lingerie and Eroticism 518 · 519

Erotic postcards. 1900
Photography began to pose a threat to drawing and became increasingly popular.

L'habitude est une seconde nature.

Xavier Sager: *Habit is Second Nature,* a postcard
for animal lovers

▲ *Mirror, Mirror.* Postcard. 1900
◄ *Lesbianism.* Postcard. 1900
► *Animal Magnetism.* A postcard for animal lovers

Honny soit, qui mal y pense!

Clients waiting in the brothels or luxury whorehouses were given albums of sexy photographs, showing the prostitutes "amusing themselves".

Clients at a brothel could select their partners by leafing through the brothel's album.

Prostitutes, album photographs

In brothels, the plump prostitutes were the most in demand... after the one-legged whore, of course...

The divide in the garment echoes the divide in the anatomy. Postcard. 1900

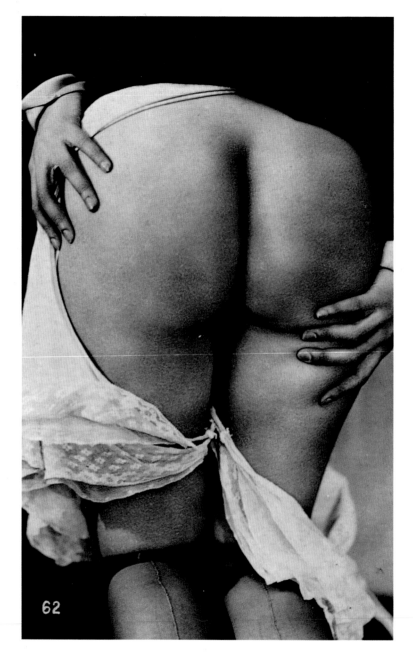

62

An ultra-fashionable item of lingerie: striped *stockings*, worn for a variety of bizarre contortions that could only be captured on camera. The practical side to divided drawers. Postcard. 1900

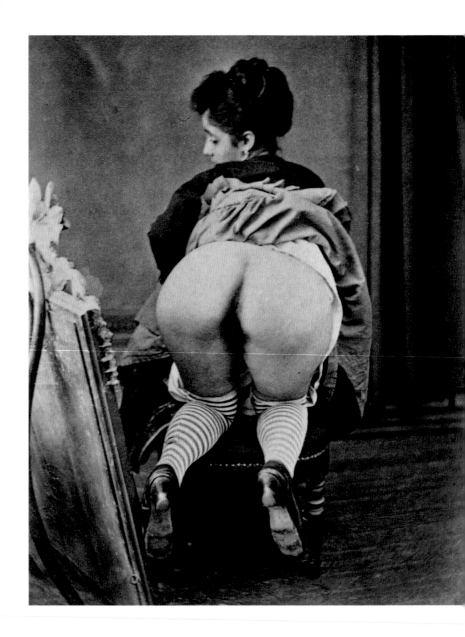

Striped Stockings. Postcards. 1900

Following pages: *Black Stockings.* Series of postcards. 1910

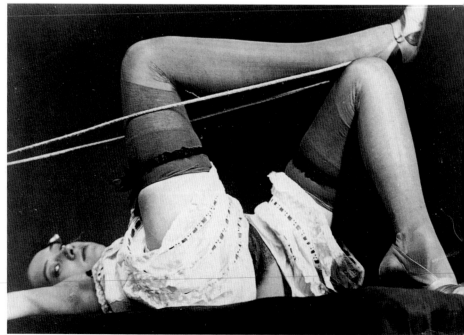

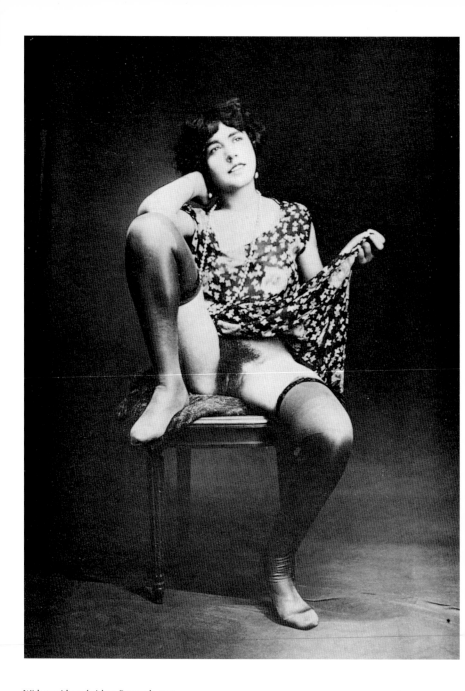

With or without *knickers*. Postcards. 1900

With or without *knickers*. Postcards. 1900

In its early days, the developing art of photography made more forays into pornography than it ever did later. Here, young women play "The Tower of Babel". Postcards. 1900

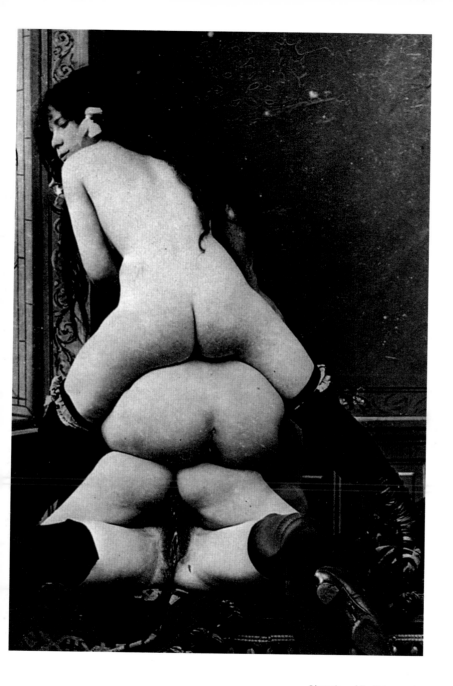

▲ The hidden delights of the *crinolin*.
▶ The revelations of *drawers* at half mast
Postcards. 1900

SÉRIE 617

Erotic postcards from the 1910s: The mirror (left) and the prey (right)

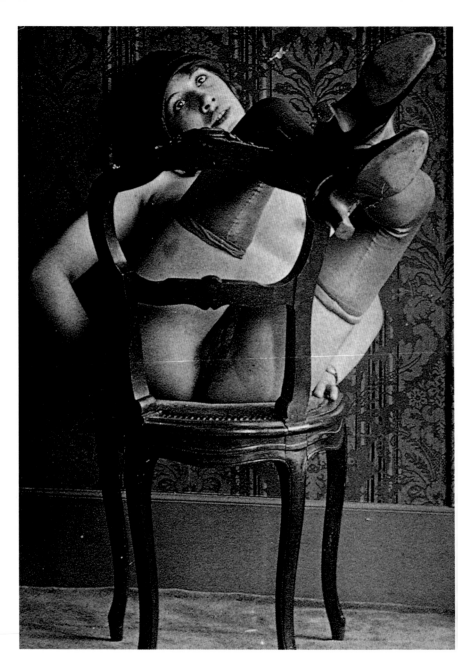

The chair was another invaluable prop for an assortment of erotic poses.
▲ *The Respectable Woman*

▲ *The French Maid.* Eroticism knew no class barriers. Postcards. 1910

"I'll show you mine, if you show me yours." Postcard. 1910

Divided *drawers*. Postcard. 1910

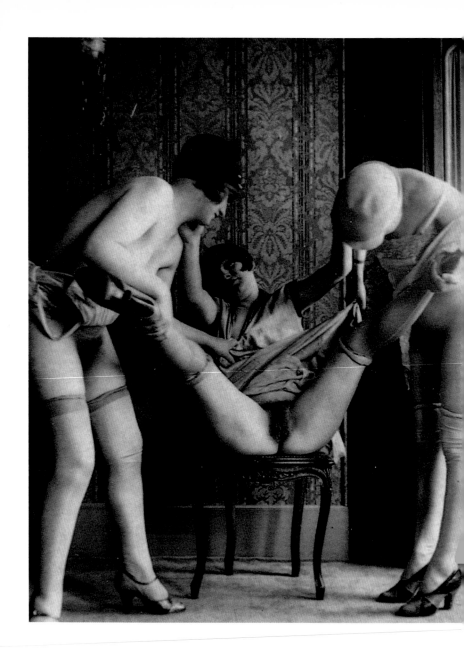

Depravity among women, a favourite theme for pornographic postcards. 1910

The Roaring Twenties and Thirties

Erotic postcards.
1920s-30s

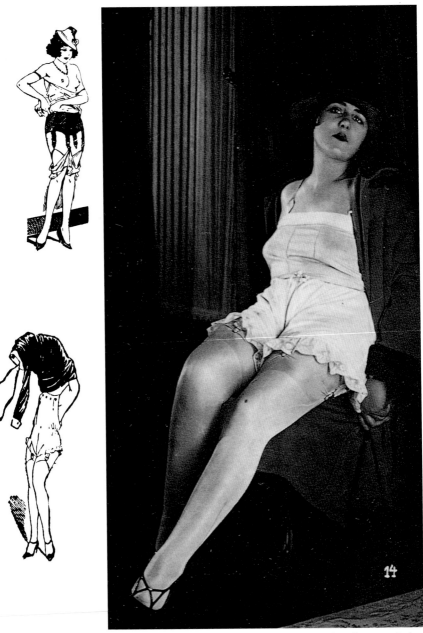

Black cotton *stockings* and divided drawers were the hallmark of eroticism in the 1900s, the Belle Epoque. In the 1920s, women let their hair down; the Roaring Twenties marked a reaction to the atrocities of the First World War. The *suspender belt* came to embody the erotic appeal of lingerie and gradually took over from the simple *garter*.

817

For a time, the two coexisted.
The lingerie sketches are by Giffey.

▲ Drawing and photo, variations on the deathless theme of the mirror. 1920s
◄ 1920s comic strips accurately depicted contemporary underwear. Here, Milton Caniff's heroine prominently
displays her wide *suspenders* in the erstwhile American comic strip.

In the 1920s-30s, photographers from Brassaï to Man Ray made their anonymous debuts with photos for erotic postcards or girlie magazines. Are these their earliest works? It is impossible to tell. Here, the recurrent theme of the mirror.

Following pages: Typical lingerie and inevitable cloche hat worn
by women in 1925

"Off to the bidet with you, ladies"... at a time when the bidet, with its removable cover, still resembled a chair. 1920s

...en by an anonymous photographer,
...e become famous...

▲ A typical *pair of knickers* with geometric flower patterns, circa 1925. In *Pour Lire à Deux*. 1930s
▶ Filmy lace drawers from the 1930s. Photo from *Pour Lire à Deux*.

Photo BRAIG

POUR LIRE à DEUX

NUMÉRO 34   MARS 1937

Reg. Com. Seine 248.570 B - ÉDITIONS-VENTE : 34, RUE GODOT DE MAUROY, PARIS 9ᵉ - Ch. Postaux Paris 1622-38

ABONNEMENT : UN AN France et Colonies 40 fr. (sous pli cacheté) 60 fr. - Étranger (sous pli cacheté) 1 £ ou 5 $

LONDON OFFICE OF « POUR LIRE A DEUX » Mr H. BONNAIRE 20 HIGH HOLBORN LONDON W. C. 1.

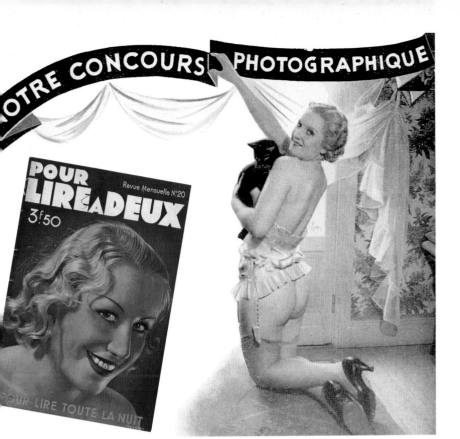

It was not only Brassaï and Man Ray who contributed to the girlie magazines of the time like *Pour Lire à Deux* or *Sex-Appeal,* but others too, such as Doisneau, Schall and Cartier-Bresson. They had to earn a crust, after all.

◄◄ An outfit half-way between surrealism and bondage, photographed by Man Ray. 1929

Lingerie and Eroticism 570 · 571

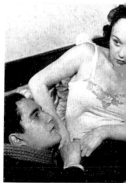

UNE HISTOIRE DE
CEINTURE

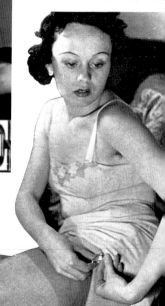

"All About Suspender Belts". Photos by Braig in
Pour Lire à Deux. 1937

Le petite

A key feature of risqué photos and one which contributed to their huge appeal was that the models were not inaccessible stars or virtual images, as they are today, but ordinary women – the girl next door, a typist – whose private moments had been caught on camera.

The accessibility of these Mrs Next-Doors did nothing to lessen their impact as objects of fantasy in the eyes of the reader or as models promoting provocative underwear in the eyes of other women. Here, for example, the Bare Breasts *bra* in *Beauté*. 1936

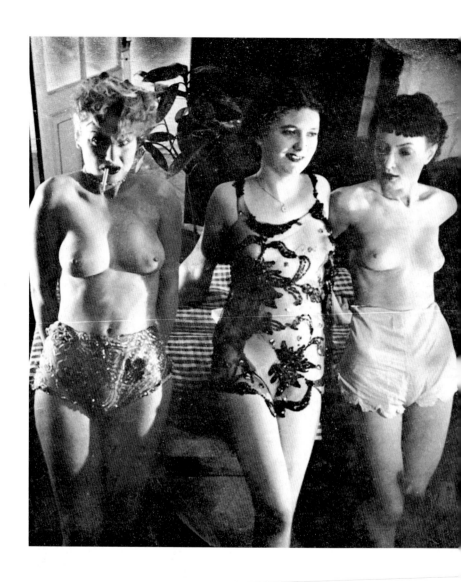

Girlie magazines of the 1930s were particularly fond of exploring the intimate relationships between women.

Mademoiselle Nicole vous offre ses curiosités galantes

Photos ultra réalistes

Scènes d'amour stupéfiantes de vérité. Ce sont des collections d'un genre très osé avec de beaux personnages en action.
Voici mes collections :

1º ELLE ET LUI .... 25 fr.
2º L'EXAMEN DE FLORA .... 25 fr.
3º SATAN CHEZ MESSALINE.... 25 fr.
4º SCÈNES GALANTES .... 25 fr.
5º LES VRAIES 32 POSITIONS .. 25 fr.
6º FRÉNÉSIES AMOUREUSES... 25 fr.
En prenant les 6 Collections ensemble .... 100 fr.
Ces collections étant très spéciales, ne peuvent être vendues qu'aux adultes seulement.

ÉCRIVEZ OU VENEZ ME VOIR

English books rares and curious

The most beautiful collection of licentious genuine english books.
SECRET PARIS (Guide of best places of entertainment in Paris)............ 25 frs
UNDER THE SKIRT, very audacious (illustrated)........................ 50 frs
THE LOVER'S PERFUMED GARDEN .... 50 frs
CARESSES, very erotical (recommanded)........................... 150 frs
Original photos of Life and Love, "real stuff" with two or more actors :
1. THE 32 BEST POSITIONS FOR LOVE .... £ 1
2. ONE MAN - TWO WOMEN...... » 1
3. MADAM AND HER MAID........ » 1
4. THE DELICIOUS PUNISHMENT » 1
The four series for £ 3 ou $ 15
Realistic films... Best models of MONT-PARNASSE and MONTMARTRE Love action films for Kodaks (8 mm and 16 mm) Pathé 9 mm. Rapid and VERY DISCREET SERVICE, letters sent out in ordinary plain envelops parcels in plain wrappers.
COME AND SEE MEE (my shop is opened from 9 a. m. to 7 p. m.).
OR WRITE TO ME discreet forwarding of goods as ordered against payment with ready money, chèque or international money-order.
Shop is open from 9 a. m. to 7 p.m., also during lunch hours.

Films spéciaux

Pris sur le vif, scènes magnifiques d'action
1º LES 32 POSES VÉCUES
2º ELLE ET LUI
3º ORGIES PRINCIÈRES
4º MESSES NOIRES
5º A QUATRE PATTES
VENEZ VOIR OU ÉCRIVEZ

Chaque film en 8 ⅜. 60 fr. — Les 5. 250 fr.
Chaque film en 9 ⅜. 80 fr. — Les 5. 325 fr.
Chaque film en 16 ⅜. 250 fr. — Les 5. 1100 fr.

Livres sur l'amour

Voici quelques titres au hasard de nos rayons :
PANTALONS DE FEMMES (illust.) 5 fr.
LE GUIDE DES CARESSES (il.) 15 fr.
LE GUIDE DES MAISONS D'AMOUR (illustré).............. 25 fr.
32 NUITS ARDENTES (illustré).... 35 fr.
CHAIRS ARDENTES (illustré)..... 35 fr.
FANNY, FILLE GALANTE........ 100 fr.
CARESSES (très recommandé)...... 100 fr.
SOUS LA BOTTE FÉMININE (ill.) 100 fr.

ÉCRIVEZ OU VENEZ ME VOIR

Caoutchouc

TOUS ARTICLES INTIMES D'HYGIÈNE pour HOMMES et FEMMES
Renseignements sur demande
à 15. - 25. - 50. et 200 fr.

Produits spéciaux

Pour triompher en amour et provoquer le "Désir" en amour. APHRODISIAQUES. Effets surprenants et sans danger (3 formes).

1º PARFUMS "ÉROTIQUES" 25 et 35 fr.
2º SUCRE-POUDRE "EXCITING" 30 fr.
3º BONBONS DRAGÉES, la boîte 25 fr.
ÉCRIVEZ OU VENEZ ME VOIR

Envoi discret par retour du courrier contre billets de banque français ou étrangers, timbres-poste français, mandats, chèques ou contre remboursement (5 fr. de supplément), sinon venez, vous recevrez le plus charmant accueil de Mlle NICOLE, vendeuse-gérante à la

LIBRAIRIE D'ANTIN
17, Rue d'Antin — PARIS-OPÉRA

In the 1920s and 1930s, the temptations on offer were endless and well-organised.
▲ Mademoiselle Nicole provided a variety of erotic books and films.

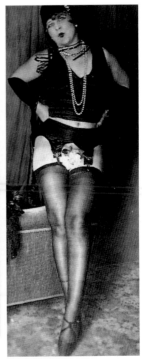

Miss Diana Slip sold devastating lingerie by mail order.
Yva Richard offered loyal customers a special collection of lingerie.
Alexandre Dupouy Collection in *Yva Richard – L'âge d'or du fétichisme*

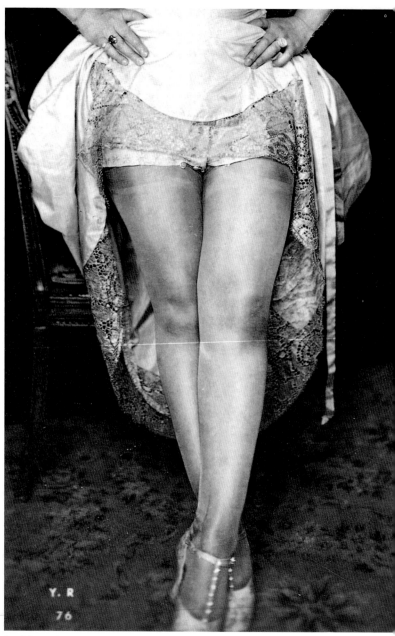

Specialist catalogues, like the girlie magazines of the 1930s, continued to fuel the fantasies of their readers by showing them what could be found under a skirt. *Yva Richard – L'âge d'or du fétichisme* by Alexandre Dupouy.

Or, as shown by *Pour Lire à Deux,* what, with a bit of luck, could be found in the Bois
de Boulogne in Paris: a sleeping beauty. 1933
Following pages: Everything you ever wanted to know about the life of a French maid

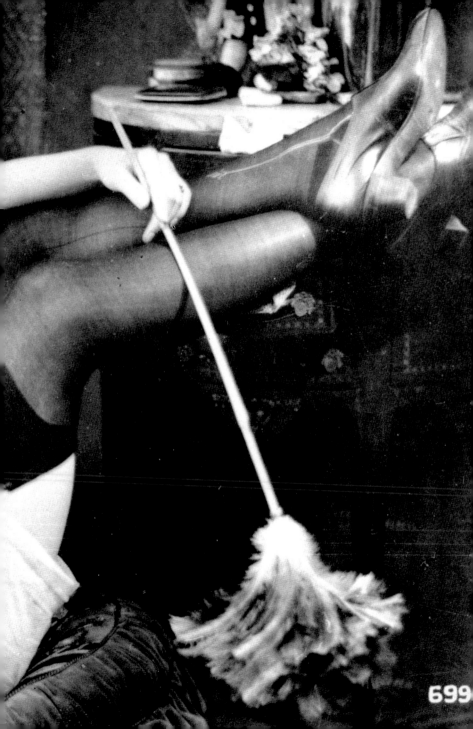

699

The private life of French maids in the 1930s: their loves, their vices, the best way of getting a wage-rise and, naturally, their lingerie.

The sex life of typists and their strategic use of underwear was also no secret.

As for respectable women, their vices and daring underwear, they followed
the lead of the inevitable *Yva Richard*. Alexandre Dupouy collection

America was not to be outdone by Europe, obeying the eternal golden rule: you can look, but don't touch.
Geo Quintana: Cover of *Movie Humor,* Hollywood girls and gags. 1938

SILK STOCKING

ories

APRIL
15c

HE LADY WRESTLES
by MARY MADDEN

HE PERSONAL TOUCH
by WARD HILL

NDID CAMERA CUT-UP
by ATWATER CULPEPPER

PETER

Peter Driben: Cover of *Silk Stockings*. 1938

The Postwar Years
1950s-60s

Look What I've Got

What a Break

Getting Your Sea Legs

A Peek-A-Knees

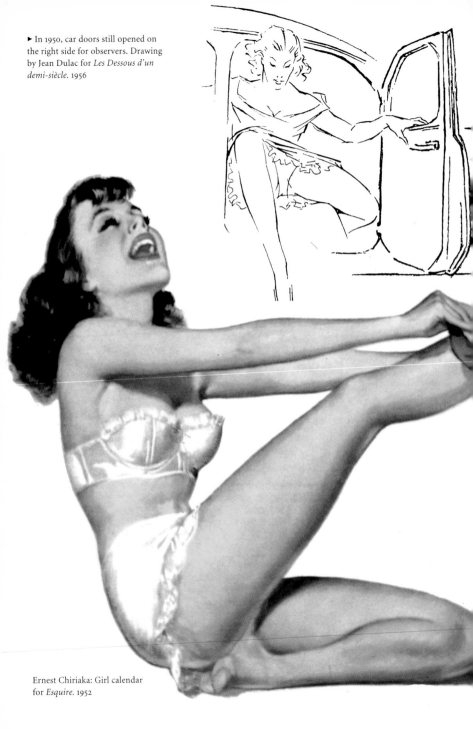

► In 1950, car doors still opened on the right side for observers. Drawing by Jean Dulac for *Les Dessous d'un demi-siècle.* 1956

Ernest Chiriaka: Girl calendar for *Esquire.* 1952

Tree for Two. Pun on the famous song "Tea for Two".
Punning postcards, Mutoscope, United States. 1945

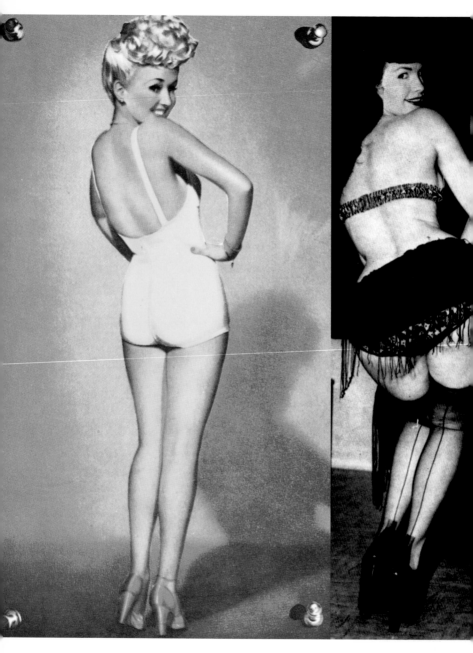

The first pin-up: Betty Grable. Her legs were insured for a million dollars. 1942. Is she wearing underwear or a swimming costume? The GIs bought 20,000 copies of this picture a week; it helped them win the Second World War.

The lovely rear view of another pin-up by Fritz Willis for *Esquire*. 1946

Betty Page, the Marilyn Monroe of erotic underwear, strikes a similar pose to that of her namesake.

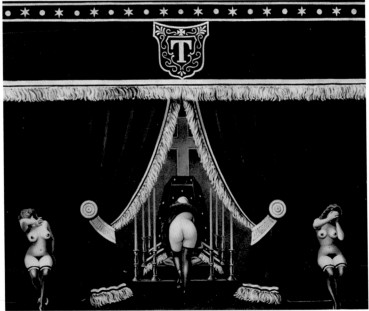

Artistes are not averse to performing in underwear.
▲ Pierre Molinier: *Dildos and Legs.* 1967
▼ Clovis Trouille: *My Funeral,* or weeping widows in black *stockings.* 1940

Hans Bellmer: *She (Him)* or the phallic *corset.* 1953

"Will Betty take Marilyn's place?" American girlie magazines from *Eyeful* to *Beauty Parade* gave her the chance in 1951.

Following pages: Betty and the man who made her, the photographer Irving Klaw, posing (left page) with his favourite models, New York. 1951-56

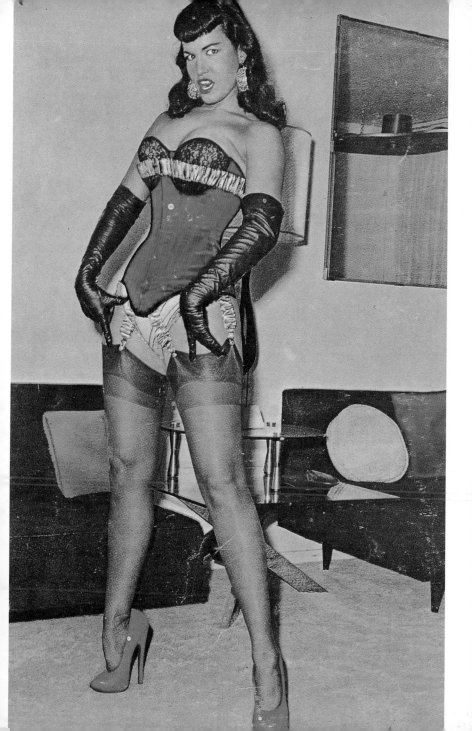

"Ah, ze nylons she take off! Weesh I owned them. I theenk my stems are bettair than Madame's, eh, boy?"

OOH, THE THINGS A FRENCH MAID SEES WHEN SHE PEEKS!

IF MADAME comes out of ze boudoir and catch naughty Marie peeping through ze keyhole, zere weel be new job open for somebody! It's ze scandal of Paree ze way Marie peek on her curvy boss, Gaby Bleu of ze Folies Bergere!

Seems like a waste of time to peek at Madame, but wise Marie say you never can tell when it might be real fun!

"Zis ees shocking! Such a shape. Like ze American cigarette, so round, so firm . . ."

...what the French Maid saw!

"Why ees eet I don't look so good in ze lace scanties like Madame?" You look pretty good, Marie gal!

"Boys, Madame's bust measurement ees a pairfect 36. Mine ees bettair . . . a pairfect 39!

Previous pages: Betty, dressed as a French maid, in *Beauty Parade.* 1955
Left and right: "Private" photos of Betty Page, New York, 1950s
Center: Photos of Betty Page by Bunny Yeager, 1955-57

Following pages: Betty, fact and fiction, in *Can Can*. 1961 (left).
Photo of Betty Page by Bunny Yeager, 1955-57 (right).

COME NASCE UNA VIGNETTA

PITTORI MODERNI

LA MODELLA
(La Realtà)

Continuiamo la serie delle vignette disegnate dal pittore O' Connor che ha per modelle donne molto avvenenti. Questa volta è in posa — nello studio del noto pittore — la stellina Genny Barner.

IL DISEGNO
(La Fantasia)

LA BATTUTA:

— E adesso la pianterà di raccontare in giro che ho le gambe storte !

Paris was also a hive of activity and the number one girlie magazine *Paris-Hollywood* took it upon itself to educate teenagers – and their fathers.
Cover of *Paris-Hollywood*. 1951

Photo for *Paris-Hollywood* by Serge Jacques – one of
the magazine's principal contributors. 1953

UN COUP DE TORCHON

CE soir là, c'est sans le moindre enthousiasme que le jeune Pierre regagnait le domicile paternel. Pourtant cette fin d'après-midi printanier aurait dû inciter a plus de gaîté. Cette sève qui se répandait si généreusement dans toute la nature inondait notre adolescent d'un vague à l'âme qui allait s'accentuant aux approches du petit pavillon familial où il ne trouverait pour l'accueillir que la vieille servante Maria. Ses parents ayant refusé de l'emmener en week-end avec eux, sous prétexte qu'il avait mieux à faire en préparant ses examens de fin d'année. Une bien brave femme cette Maria, mais qui s'obstinait à le traiter comme le bébé qu'elle avait connu vingt ans plus tôt, ce qui avait le don de l'exaspérer. En entrant dans la maison il fit le moins de bruit possible pour ne pas signaler sa présence et monta directement dans sa chambre afin de pouvoir travailler tranquillement avant l'heure du dîner. Il eut la surprise de trouver cette pièce dans le désordre où il l'avait laissée, son lit n'était même pas fait. Tout en se déshabillant, puis en enfilant son pyjama, il ne cessait de maugréer contre

The housewife according to *Paris-Hollywood*. Her weapons: broomstick and suspender-belt…

cette Maria même plus capable de remplir
son office. Après avoir hésité, il l'appelle et
s'installe à sa table de travail tout en bou-
gonnant. C'est d'un son qui tient plus d'un
aboiement que d'une voix humaine qu'il
crie « Entrez! », en réponse à quelques
coups discrets frappés à la porte, et sans se
retourner, commence à exprimer de la
façon la plus véhémente son indignation.
Mais cette attaque reste sans réponse. Il
se retourne d'une pièce et manque choir de
saisissement... Est-il la proie d'une halluci-
nation?... d'un mirage? Au lieu de la vieille
Maria, vêtue de pilou, aux cheveux poivre
et sel, au nez adorné d'une verrue, et aux
sourcils broussailleux... Il a devant lui la
plus charmante des apparitions. A faire
pâlir de jalousie toutes les stars dont les
portraits ornent sa chambre... Il n'a jamais
rien vu de si blond, de si rose, de si frais, de
si gracieux et de si coquin !... Et quel voix
adorable jaillit de cette bouche... Pour lui
expliquer que la délicieuse inconnue s'appelle Suzy... qu'elle est une nièce de Maria
laquelle appelée télégraphiquement à son
pays, l'a arrachée au petit bistrot familial
pour lui confier la garde du pavillon et de
son jeune maître. Suzy s'excuse auprès de
Pierre de ne pas avoir eu le temps de faire
la chambre, mais qu'elle allait revenir de
suite pour réparer cette omission. Puis elle
quitte la pièce, laissant dans son sillage un
parfum qui ne quitte plus notre jeune étu-
diant... Cette aventure dont il rêve depuis
qu'il a l'âge d'aimer, il la sent maintenant à
sa portée. Une timidité naturelle et un
grand respect de la discipline familiale en
fait de lui l'émule bien involontaire du
rosier de madame Husson ». Mais, si en
pratique il a toutes les retenues, en imagination il a toutes les audaces, et les aven-
tures de Don Juan, Casanova et autres
grands amoureux n'ont plus de secrets pour
lui. En attendant le retour de Suzy il relit
attentivement un chapitre particulièrement
évocateur. Aussi, est-ce l'esprit plein d'images libertines qu'il va ouvrir à la jeune
femme de chambre. Celle-ci vêtue d'un

The girls who appeared in *Paris-Hollywood* wore provocative underwear, but, like angels, had no sex. This was because pubic hair was censored and showing it was punishable by prison. It was removed with an airbrush. Here,

original photos, which have not been retouched, by Serge Jacques for the magazine. 1954
Following pages: Double page spread from *Paris-Hollywood*. 1955

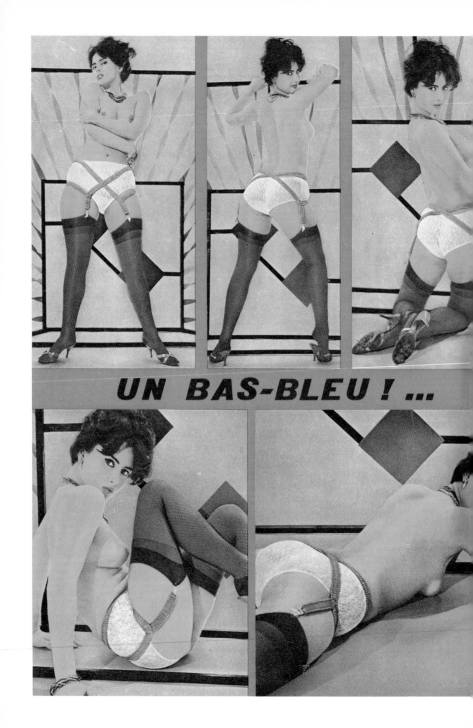

UN BAS-BLEU ! ...

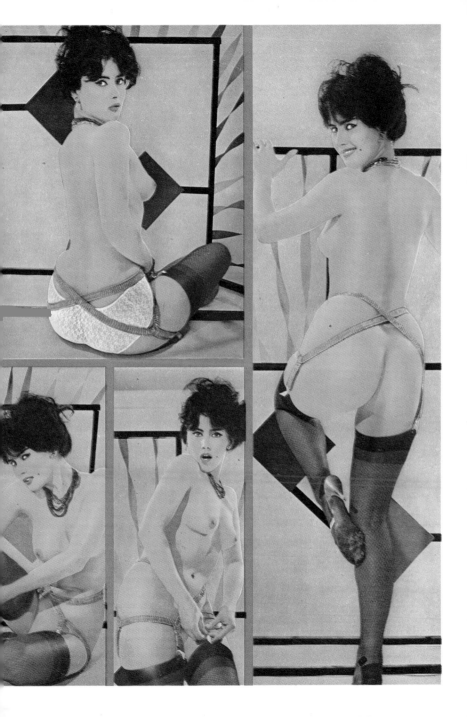

Unretouched bottoms from *Paris-Hollywood*. Photos by Serge Jacques. 1950s

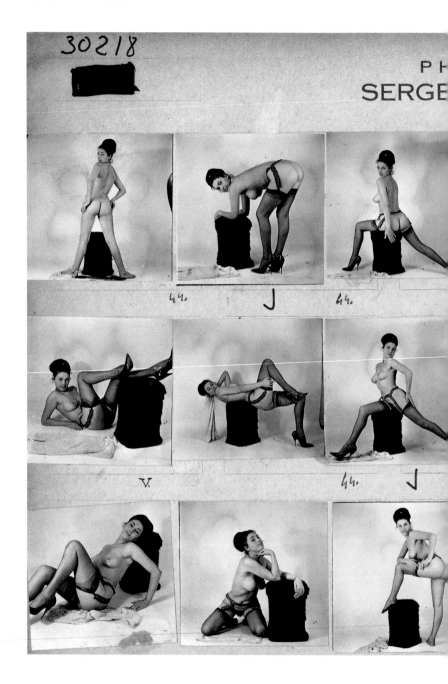

Typical poses, enabling *Paris-Hollywood* to illustrate any story line. Photos by Serge Jacques. 1952

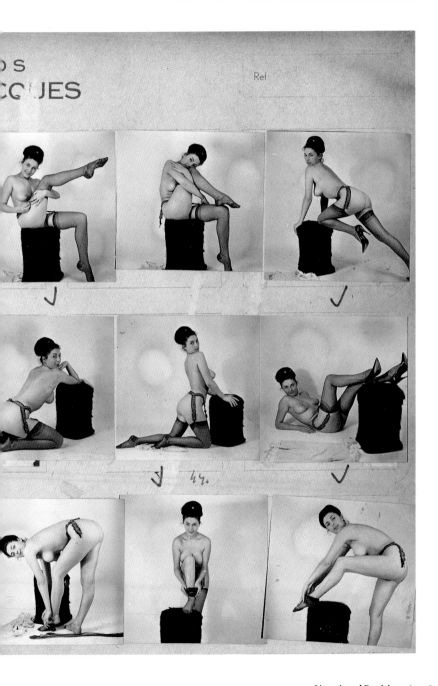

The complicated, but extremely alluring, underwear of the *Paris-Hollywood* girls. Photos by Serge Jacques. 1950s

Cover (back and front) of an issue of *Paris-Hollywood*. 1955

Folies de
PARIS ET DE
HOLLYWOOD

N° 467
PRIX :
5 F

ARAIT DEUX FOIS PAR MOIS 3 PAGES
UBLICATION INTERDITE A L'AFFICHAGE
T A LA VENTE AUX MINEURS DE 18 ANS
PRIX ÉTRANGER : 6 F

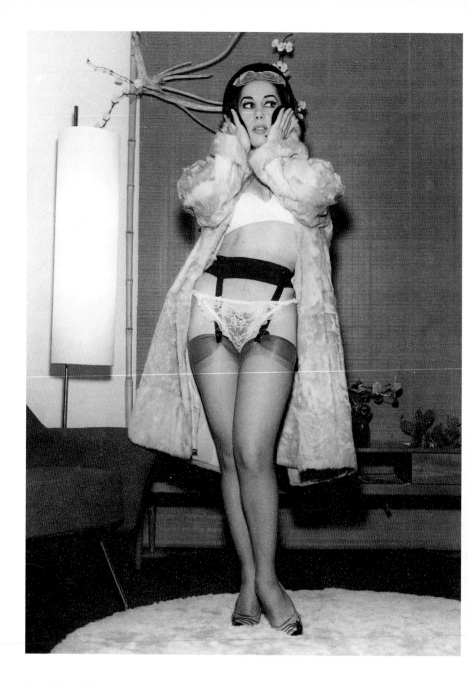

Paris-Hollywood girl. Serge Jacques Collection. 1958

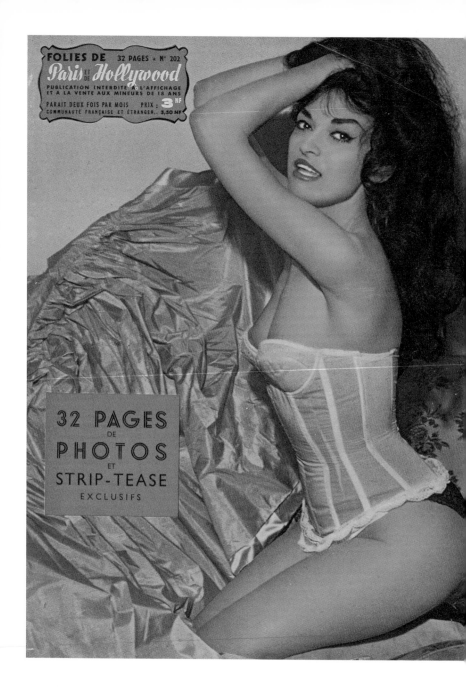

FOLIES DE 32 PAGES ★ N° 202

Paris ET DE *Hollywood*

PUBLICATION INTERDITE A L'AFFICHAGE
ET A LA VENTE AUX MINEURS DE 18 ANS

PARAIT DEUX FOIS PAR MOIS · PRIX : 3 NF
COMMUNAUTÉ FRANÇAISE ET ÉTRANGER.. 3,50 NF

32 PAGES
DE
PHOTOS
ET
STRIP-TEASE
EXCLUSIFS

Cover of *Paris-Hollywood*. 1954

The provocative *waspie* in *Paris-Hollywood*.
Photo by Serge Jacques. 1959

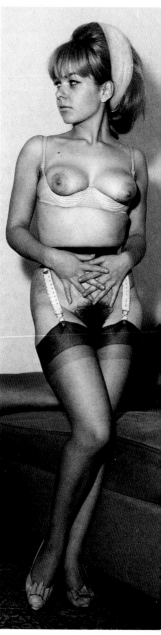

Garments necessary and unnecessary. Serge Jacques Collection. 1956-57

▲ Playing the perfect secretary, one of
the girls from the Crazy Horse club, the
Parisian temple of striptease

▶ The *Amazone,* Crazy
Horse-style. Photos by
Serge Jacques. 1959

The *Paris-Hollywood* collection and the Serge Jacques Collection form an invaluable erotic anthology of women's lingerie in the 1950s-60s.

PARIS SEXI

Secret's Girls

Nº 1 MENSUEL
★ 150 Francs ★

MOI ET TOI

NON INTERDIT A L'AFFICHAGE

MENSUEL
150 Francs

VOTRE PARIS

SECRET GIRLS of PARIS!

MENSUEL
Nº 2 ★ 150 fr.

SECRET

PARIS TOUJOURS PARIS

MENSUEL
PRIX : 150 Francs

▲ Some of *Paris-Hollywood*'s many competitors. 1954-56
◀ Serge Jacques for *Paris-Tabou*. 1960s

Taschen has published a comprehensive book on American girlie magazines of the 1960s.
Following pages: Photos of underwear by Elmer Batters. 1960s

W OLD ARE YOU SEXUALLY?

WHISPER

NOV.
25¢

EDRINE PARTIES • CAN YOU STAND TORTURE?

TO BENEDIKT
BEST REGARDS

The simple, provocative works of an American fetishist photographer, Elmer Batters, alias "Mr Black Silk Stockings", also called "Mr Foot" due to his other obsession. 1960s. In *Elmer Batters. From the Tip of the Toes to the Top of the Hose*, Taschen. 1995

Elmer Batters: Feet and buttocks. 1960s

"Fifty dollars a day" is what Elmer Batters paid his models in the 1960s-70s.

The *knickers* worn by "Lolitas" drive Japanese men wild.
▲ The typist behind her large Japanese typewriter, wearing sensible Petit Bateau *knickers*. Photo by Gilles Néret. 1960s ◄ Cover of a soft-porn magazine. 1960s. Western underwear invaded Japan after the war, taking the place of the only lingerie worn under a kimono: ribbons.

The height of eroticism for Japanese men: schoolgirls in uniform displaying their strange foreign underwear.
Photo by Gilles Néret. 1960s

別冊 笑の泉
ユーモア
＆ グラフ

すてきな美女が勢揃い
新年豪華グラフ決定版

娘ざかり初春の粧い
お嬢さんの新春絵日記

続・セーラー服の処女
乙女の肌

美人ドライバー
裸で乗り初め

女カメラマン
かわいい覗き屋

禁男のカルタ会
一枚一枚とりましょう

恋に悶える若女将
夜ひらく花

バス・ルームの美女
ピンクの湯気につつまれて

総天然色特大口絵
アメリカ娘のお座敷タッチ
"晴着を脱いでおめでとう"

シカラーロ絵（マンスリー・マスコット）
チャーム・カレンダー

新年特大号 おとそ気分初すがたチラチラ特集

Cover of a popular weekly magazine. 1960s

In Japan pubic hair is still taboo, being a strange, uncouth sign of womanhood (Japanese women from good families are usually almost hairless, having removed unwanted body hair from time immemorial). *Knickers* are thus regarded

as very tasteful and have found a home from home.
Photos by Gilles Néret. 1960s

Young Japanese women are not ashamed to show off their foreign underwear, in the same way as they might a holiday souvenir.
▲ This schoolgirl does not need to be asked twice to display her underwear.

▲ Bus conductor, proudly showing her underwear to the West
Photos by Gilles Néret. 1960s

In the space of a decade, the 1960s, Japanese women discovered the entire history of Western underwear, from the *garter* to *hold-ups*.
Here, the pianist's *garter*. Photo by Gilles Néret. 1960s

Today in Japan, Western underwear, which in the 1960s was an object of interest, is now a mainstay of the sex industry, and the "Lolitas" of the 1990s make pocket money by selling their *briefs,* preferably used, in the small ads. "I've also sold my saliva" boasted the schoolgirl on the right. 1997

So the *Gaijin Dame,* the wicked foreigners, have infected Japan with the virus of Western underwear. But, by copying it, then improving it, as is their wont, the Japanese have turned the tables on the West and, now, one women out of four in the world will be wearing underwear made in Japan.

▲ Gilles Néret, representing several French labels, doing a demonstration in a Tokyo department store, Seibu. 1961

▲ Stockings that never wear out, made of Teijin fibre; three for
the price of one. Photo by Xavier-G.N. 1995

The End of a Millennium
1970s-90s

In the last decades of this century, women have become warriors, like Vampirella, or inaccessible, like the bunny girls in *Playboy*. The girls-next-door have been replaced by space-women from another planet and their aggressive underwear-outerwear doubles as armour.
From left to right: José Gonzalez: Vampirella, powerful and dangerous, but also delicate and sensitive – just like the modern woman – in her sexy *leotard*. 1976. Don Lewis: Three bunny girls dressed to please for *Playboy*. 1966-67

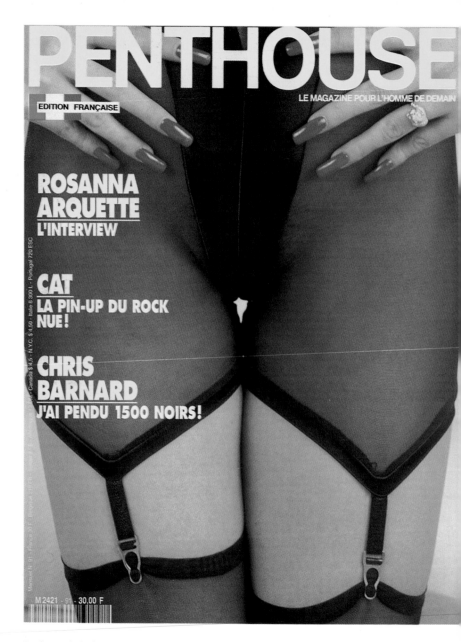

PENTHOUSE

LE MAGAZINE POUR L'HOMME DE DEMAIN

EDITION FRANÇAISE

ROSANNA ARQUETTE
L'INTERVIEW

CAT
LA PIN-UP DU ROCK NUE!

CHRIS BARNARD
J'AI PENDU 1500 NOIRS!

M 2421 - 91 - 30.00 F

Penthouse, Playboy's great rival, is less hypocritical and has been more successful in keeping pace with the times, by becoming harder
▲ Cover. 1992 ► "Packaging" for underwear, typical of *Penthouse.* 1995

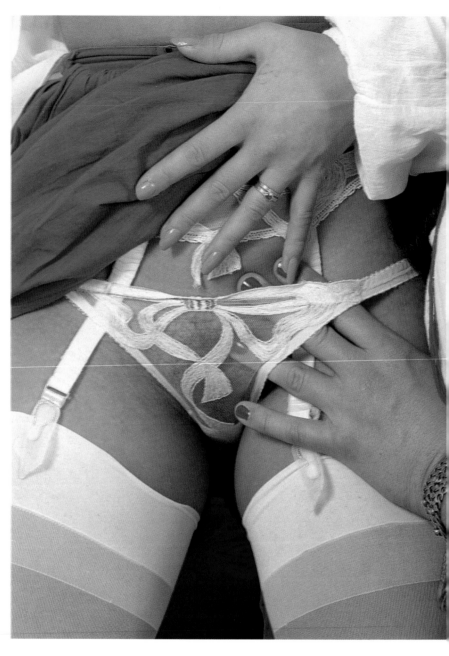

A favourite theme in erotic magazines: lesbianism. The hand working its way inside the *briefs* belongs to another woman. Photo by Sarah Joyce. 1980s

Two fantasies are better than one. Here, lesbianism and retro-style lingerie. Photo by Sarah Joyce. 1980s
Following pages: Portraying a beautiful and defenceless odalisque is one way of reassuring the American
reader who is, with good reason, afraid of his wife. Photo by Sarah Joyce. 1980s

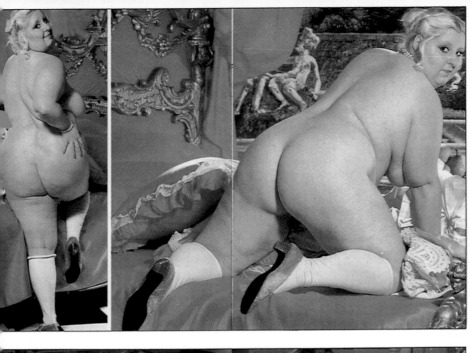

Hustler, unlike other magazines in the 1980s, made it a point of honour to shock its readers. The end always justified the means: Rubens-style obesity (top), or furs (bottom).

Hustler was the first magazine to show pregnant women indulging in sexual activities (top) and to depict bestiality (bottom).

THE BANQUET

Other fantasies exploited by *Hustler* were the fascination of Americans for the provocative prints of the 18th century and the depravity of the Age of Louis XIV or the liking of paedophiles for "Lolitas" and other baby-faced girls. Following pages: Fantasy in uniform, or naughty nurses on parade. In *Lui,* the French *Playboy* of the 1980s

The fantasy of the bride. Photos by Serge Jacques. 1993-94

Following pages: The fantasy of religious taboos. Photo by Serge Jacques. 1994

BRIGITTE NIELSEN

▲ The fantasy of lesbians in the shower. Photos by Serge Jacques. 1995
◄ Draped with chains that are more protective than aggressive, Brigitte Nielsen, former Mrs Rambo, embodies the type of assertive woman who is a product of the late 20th century. 1997

The fantasy of the defenceless victim: Sarah White, the queen of porn in the 1990s, photographed by Dahmane, the inventor of Porn-Art. 1993

The American photographer Eric Kroll is attracted by superwomen and other dominant "vixens" capable of using their entire armoury of weapons, including underwear.
▲ Exquisite lingerie, USA, 1995 ▶ *Tights* and high-heeled shoes for masochistic fetishists. 1996

The confident, assertive modern woman, as seen by Eric Kroll, with the added phantasm of an Indian squaw disguise. Photos published in *Fetish Girls,* Taschen. 1994

The art of striptease, which draws its origins from 19th-century acts like the "Coucher d'Yvette" in Paris, a great favourite with Toulouse-Lautrec and his friends, reached its apogee in the United States. It then crossed back over the Atlantic and set up strip joints in all the capitals of Europe. Here, the famous Crazy Horse in Paris, shortly after it opened. 1950s

Jennie Lee

Besides her duly-recorded claim to having the biggest bust in burlesque—a phenomenal 42 inches—she also performs remarkable maneuvers with well-placed tassles.

In the 1950s, in the United States, the fashion for abnormally large breasts reached epic proportions, foreshadowing the current fashion for silicone implants. Jennie Lee, a burlesque star of the time, was a huge success twirling her tassels every which way.

During the same period, in America, striptease became more democratic. To rekindle their husbands' ardour, wives could go to special schools to learn how to strip, using provocative lingerie like true professionals. Here, a teacher shows them the ropes. 1950s

Following pages: To meet growing demand, a former striptease artiste of repute, the French-sounding Lili St Cyr, successfully launched her mail-order firm, selling sexy lingerie to wives. Europe followed suit.

Lili St. Cyr

#948 STRIP STAR
Sequin studded G-String
and pasties. Black or Red.
Sizes: S·M·L **$12.95 per set**

FROM THE COLLECTION OF
ERIC KROLL 212-684-2465

F. 92683

#305 LACE ALLURE
Flowing yards of nylon lace veil you
luxuriously. Black lace only.
Sizes: S·M·L **$24.95**

#330 LOVE GODDESS
Cloud drift cover-up of
sheerest nylon. Black only.
Sizes: S·M·L **$14.95**

Be sure to visit our Shoe Boutique at:
12812 GARDEN GROVE BLVD., SUITE G, GARDEN GROVE, CA. 92643

**#420 BLACK LEATHER
OOK SLING BRA**
izes: 32-40 A-D cups **$6.95**

**422 BALCK LEATHER
OOK GARTER BELT**
izes: 22-30" waist. **$6.95**

**#210 ON DISPLAY
SLING BRA**
Sheer nylon.
Black or Nude.
Sizes: 32-40
A-D cups. **$5.95**

**#220 SHEER DEAR
GARTER BELT**
Sheer nylon.
Black or Nude.
Sizes: 22-30" waist.
$5.95

**#100 MOULIN ROUGE
FRENCH BRA**
Black lace only.
Sizes: 22-30" waist **$6.95**

**#285 L'AUTRE SOIR
GARTER BELT**
Black lace only
Sizes: 22-30" waist. **$6.95**

#83 COUVERT G-STRING
Black lace only.
Sizes: 22-30" waist. **$2.50**

#610 SAVAGE EVE BRA
Leopard only. Sizes: 32-40
A-D cups. **$6.95**

**#615 ADAM'S FALL
GARTER BELT**
Leopard only.
Sizes: 22-30" waist. **$6.95**

**#65 LEAST OF ALL
G-STRING**
Leopard only. Sizes: 22-30"
waist. **$2.50**

#117 LEATHER LOVI
2 Piece bikini looks just
like real leather. Black c
Sizes: S-M-L. **$8.95**

**#480 HOLLYWOOD
HOLD UP**
Leather look sling bra
that laces in front to
adjust the amount of
cleavage. Black only.
Sizes: 32-40 A-D cups.
$7.95

**#485 LINE TAMER
BODY CINCHER**
Adjustable leather look,
front lacing cincher has
6 detachable garters to
hold up our opera hose
(Shown) Black only. Sizes:
22-30" waist. **$16.95**

#425 LITTLE SINNER
Leather look G-string.
Black only. Sizes: 22-30"
waist. **$2.50**

**#26 BLACK DIAMOND
OPERA HOSE**
Lili's exclusive hip
length opera hose
Black only.
Sizes: 8½ - 11
$5.95

#114-3 RING CIRCUS
Leather look romper. 3 rings
hold it in place. Black only
Sizes: S-M-L. **$10.95**

#94 LEATHER VIXEN
Almost nothing halter and
micro-mini wrap skirt of
washable leather look nylon.
Black only. Sizes: S-M-L. **$10.95**

#430 SEX QUEEN
Leather look siren style
halter dress. Black only.
Sizes: 8-16. **$16.95**

OBSESSION

Une création prestigieuse. Comme deux grands yeux ouverts cernés de noir, des seins aux bouts qui pointent au travers de bonnets transparents. Un soutien-gorge excentrique à double armature, à bretelles de dentelle, au dos en Lycra. Une pierre qui brille entre les seins.

COULEUR : noir.

TAILLES : 70 à 85 (3 à 7).

N° 2516   Prix : **72 F**

Léger voile transparent, c'est le slip assorti aux 40 petites pierres disposées en triangle. Il complète cet ensemble sensationnel.

COULEUR : noir.

TAILLES : 38 à 46.

N° **2519**   Prix : **33 F**

CINQ A SEPT

Eh ! oui... avec ce fascinant shorty vous connaîtrez des cinq à sept étourdissants. Avez-vous remarqué sa coupe originale, et les fanfreluches qui en font le piquant : le galon scintillant qui borde le plastron et la petite jupette, les deux fleurs en rosace, le petit nœud à la taille, le large ruban noué sous la nuque. Conçu avec un petit slip, ce modèle peut se porter également comme nuisette.

Perlon 20 den.

COULEUR : noir.

TAILLES : 38 à 48.

N° **3051**   Prix : **49 F**

RUSSIA

Toujours une poitrine magnifique. Côtés, dos, bretelles, et bande sous les bonnets, sont en tissus élastiques. De fines dentelles disposées, harmonieusement, donnent un grand chic à ce soutien-gorge. Perlon et Lycra.

COULEUR : rouge, dentelle noire.

TAILLES : 70 à 90.

N° **2239**   Prix : **59 F**

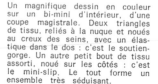

Pour votre joie de vivre, portez des modèles
      ADELINE

FROSY

Un magnifique dessin en couleur sur un bi-mini d'intérieur, d'une coupe magistrale. Deux triangles de tissu, reliés à la nuque et noués au creux des seins, avec un élastique dans le dos : c'est le soutien-gorge. Un autre petit bout de tissu assorti, noué sur les côtés : c'est le mini-slip. Le tout forme un ensemble très séduisant.

COULEUR : voir photo.

TAILLES : 38 à 48.

N° **3082**   Prix : **59 F**

Adeline

3028

Prix : 4?

NUIT DE REVE. Une magnifique chemise de nuit, une perles de notre collection. Un décolleté très prof coquettement entrouvert sur la poitrine, bordé d somptueuse dentelle argentée. Un tissu transparent, ple et léger, ourlé de fines dentelles. Ce modèle vous rendra plus belle, plus désirable.

Perlon 20 den. Couleur : rose. Tailles : 38 à 48.

3049

HARMONIE. Vous serez très belle dans cet ensemble pantalon, très décoleté, en Hélanca élastique. Il est pratique, une fermeture éclair descend de la poitrine jusqu'à dix centimètres dans le dos. Il galbe merveilleusement votre corps, il donne une 'grande allure à votre silhouette. Filet Hélanca. Couleur : noir. Tailles : 38 à 48.

Prix : 67 F ▶

3010

PASSION. Toute femme à la page possède au moins un bi-mini de nuit. Si vous n'en avez pas encore, vous choisirez ce magnifique modèle. La coupe en est osée, mais l'ornementation somptueuse. Le slip ouvert devant et le soutien-gorge se ferment grâce à d'élégants nœuds de ruban. Les deux pieces, aux riches dessins de fleurs, sont bordées d'une fine dentelle. Perlon. Couleur : voir photo. Tailles : 38 à 48.

Prix : 38 F ▼

3036

PLACE PIGALLE. Slip ouvert. Spirituel et séduisant. Dentelle Perlon doublée Perlon Charmeuse. Couleur : noir sur fond rouge. Tailles : 38 à 48.

Prix : 33 F ▼

3013

PAPILLON. Mini-slip en satin brillant. Satin. Couleur : noir. Tailles : 38 à 48.

Prix : 30 F ▼

PLACE PIGALLE

PAPILLON

3035

Nr. 2185

Nr. 3034

3035 - 2185 et 3034

scriptions

page 14

MINOUCHE

Exquise chemise-culotte. Elle donne une ligne admirable. Elle moule parfaitement, mais laisse une grande liberté de mouvement. Elle est en detelle Helanca, ajustée par une fermeture éclair sur le devant. Son soutien-gorge incorporé laisse la poitrine très découverte.
Dentelle Helanca.
COULEUR : noir.
TAILLES : 38 à 48.

N° **3039**   Prix : **129 F**

SLIP-TRIANGLE

Un petit slip bien coupé.
COULEUR : rouge, noir ou chair.
TAILLES : 38 à 48.

N° **3042**   Prix : **10 F**

BAS-HELANCA

Ce bas « haute-mode » complètera heureusement votre toilette. Il ne glisse pas, maintenu très haut par une jarretière de dentelle, piquée d'une rose rouge. Qualité exceptionnelle.
Helanca.
COULEUR : noir.
TAILLES : 8 à 11.

N° **3041**   Prix : **48 F**

Nr. 3039

A stripper working on a client after her spot in a Parisian nightclub. 1962

In certain states in the USA, it was against the law for strippers to show
their breasts. This problem could easily be avoided, as a surprisingly lifelike
plastic mould was enough to create an illusion of bare flesh. The police were
helpless and the audience could see nothing in the glare of the lights. A.F.P
document. 1960s

LILI DE SAIGON
DU SEXY

LILI DE SAIGON
FICHE SIGNALÉTIQUE.
Nationalité française.
AGE : 26 ans.
CHEVEUX : bruns.
YEUX : noisette.
TAILLE : 1,65 m.
POIDS : 54 kg.
TOUR DE POITRINE : 90 cm.
TOUR DE HANCHES : 90 cm.

Other stars, other famous striptease joints:
▲ Lily de Saigon at the Sexy
▶ Seymour in the same nightclub. Photos published in *Paris-Hollywood*. 1960s

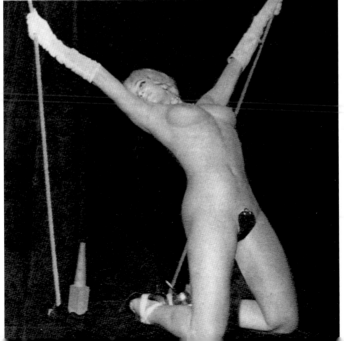

Allen Jones: Designs inspired by
"Gone with the Wind", for British
Television, 1971. Or the lingerie worn
by Southern Belle, Scarlett, and
reinterpreted by the Pop artist…

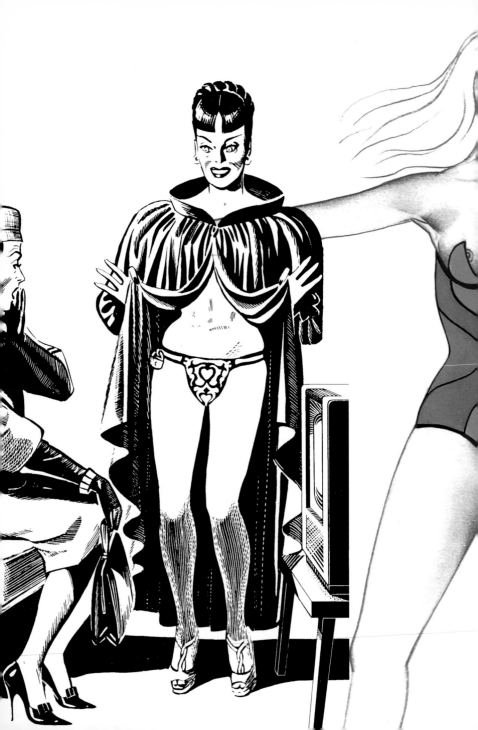

◄ Drawing by Eric Stanton: *The Chastity Belt,* 1959, which inspired certain outfits, opposite, for the film Allen Jones made for British television in 1971.

Since the 1970s the Crazy Horse has become redoubtably efficient, with numbers as strictly choreographed as the Bolshoi Ballet and lighting effects drawing virtual underwear on the dancers' naked bodies. It has also opened up clubs throughout the world.

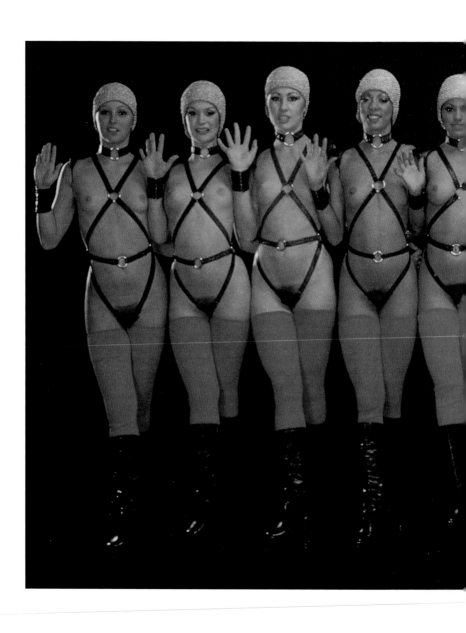

The army of girls at the Crazy Horse on parade. Nudes are an integral part of the show, but vestigial underwear, such as these *straps,* are still worn for erotic effect, emphasising breasts, hips and pubes. 1990s

EXCITING
Holly-nites
frederick's
OF HOLLYWOOD

A

STRAIGHT FROM HOLLYWOOD

J

24 CARAT GOLD TRIM

B

TIME PAYMENTS
See Page **16**

H

I

TREASURE CHEST TRIMMED IN GENUINE, 24 CARAT GOLD!

G

C

PANTIE... ROBE... BABY DOLL ...ALL ONLY $8.98

K

E

F

FASCINATING FREDERICK'S STYLING IN FABULOUS LUREX

N

L

NEW! NEW! NEW!

D

$4.98

O

M

2 for $5.88

N #3764 THE FRINGE
Fantabulous little nothing of a pantie in naughty nylon... rayon fringe adds fascination. Black, Red or White. Waist sizes 22" to 30". $2.98

O #875 LOVELY LACE
Nylon lace Bikini. Hanky size panties are NEW! White Frost or Spicy Black Pearl. 22" to 30" waist. Each $2.98

2 for $5.88

IT'S 24 CARAT GOLD JERSEY!

*C*USTOM VICTORIAN *C*ORSETS

In the USA, different mail-order firms specialise in different types of sexy underwear.

▲ For B. R. Créations, the erotic *corset* has to be Victorian. 1990

◄ Frederick's of Hollywood supplies underwear as worn by the stars. 1995

"The Invention" by chemist Jean Parat, designed for "worried fathers and husbands". Circa 1900

Iron *chastity-belts*. 16th century

The iron *chastity belt*, the first sadomasochistic undergarment, has been handed down through the ages and is even more of a hit today in vinyl form.

The *chastity belt* in 1930

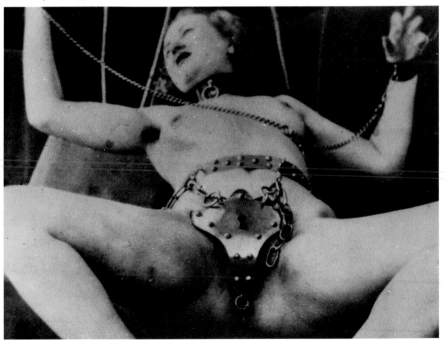

Over the centuries, underwear has often caused women to suffer, albeit of their own free will. At the hands of sadomasochists, undergarments have been transformed into kinky instruments of torture. But, in sex games, victim and torturer are obviously in league with each other. The roles can also be reversed and, in this master-slave

relationship, it is impossible to say who is the slave and who the master.

▲ Chained beauties. In *L'Etude Académique*. 1895

◄ Anonymous Flemish print, *La Bellifortis, chastity belt* and its key. 16th century

Anonymous: Sadomasochistic iron *corset*, or revamping the Middle Ages. 1900s

Sadomasochistic outfit made of metal. 1933

Sadomasochistic depravity in the Roaring Twenties: whips, padlocked *G-strings,* and *garters* or *suspenders* that resemble chains.

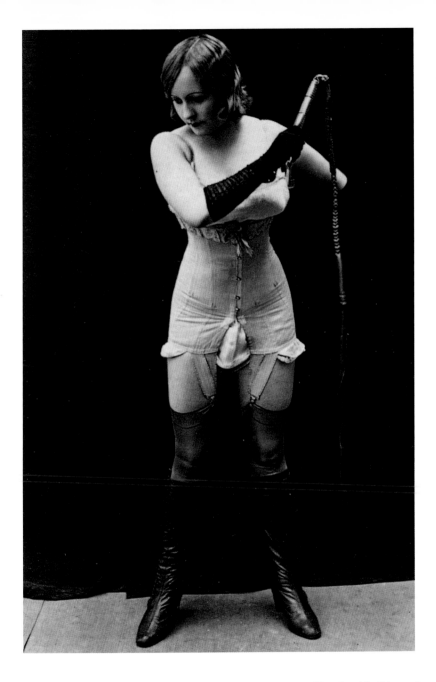

SM underwear from the 1920s was not made of vinyl but of shiny materials, patent leather or moleskin, probably to create the impression of the metal once used for *chastity belts*.

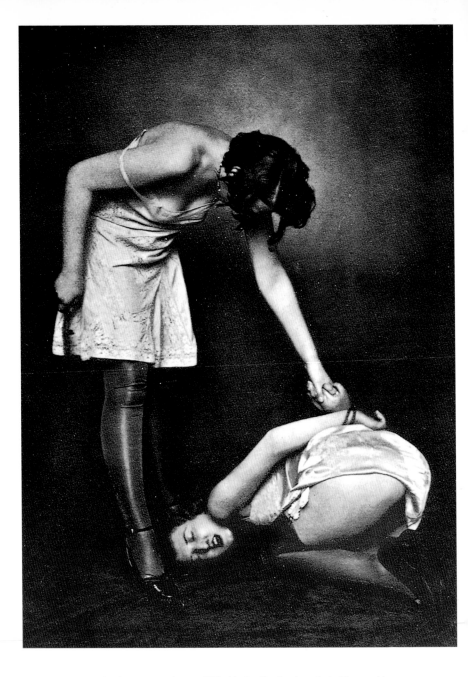

SM in Germany is no laughing matter. Photos published in *Der Flagellantismus in der Photographie.* 1933

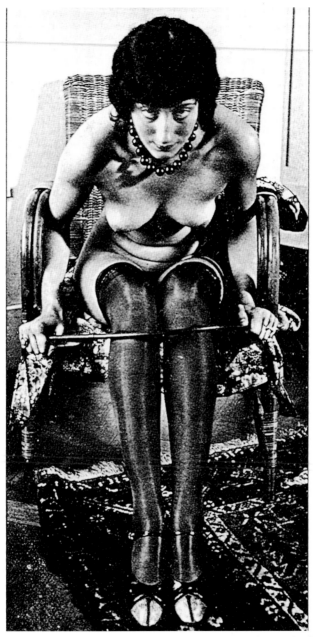

Following pages: Anonymous, *The Punishment,* or SM in schools. Although taken in the 1920s, the photo has an old-fashioned feel, due to the extremely practical divided drawers, of which the photographer seems to have found an abundant supply.

Corsets, laces, black *stockings:* SM underwear of the 1920s-30s clearly draws its inspiration from the fantasies and memories of a reinvented past.

Carlo: Illustration (above) and cover (left page) for a pre-war fetishist novel, *The Modern Inquisitor,* or the cruelty and humiliation inflicted on a young woman prisoner by a cruel nobleman from Spain, worthy of the Inquisition. 1930s

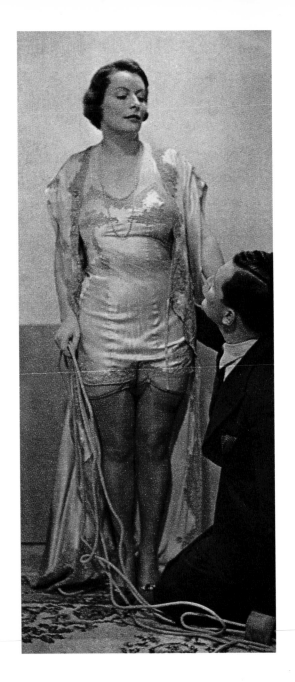

The Mistress, in every sense of the word. In *Paravent.* 1933

Bondage outfit in fishing twine, a must for a good catch.
In *Pour Lire à Deux.* 1930s

Drawing by Gene Bilbrew: SM chastity outfit, complete with
padlocks and key. 1956

Other 1950s versions of *chastity belts* (above and top left).
The more leather straps and metal buckles, the better.

Whipping is no good without the requisite lingerie. And French maids' caps and uniforms are not to be spurned... 1958

Eric Stanton: Chic (voyeurism) and shock (a whipping in fashionable circles).
Late 1950s

▲ Drawing by Eneg in *Exotique,* an SM magazine. 1962
► Cover by Gene Bilbrew for *Exotique.* 1962
In the early 1960s, shapes became sharper-edged, with breasts honed to a fine point.

Exotique

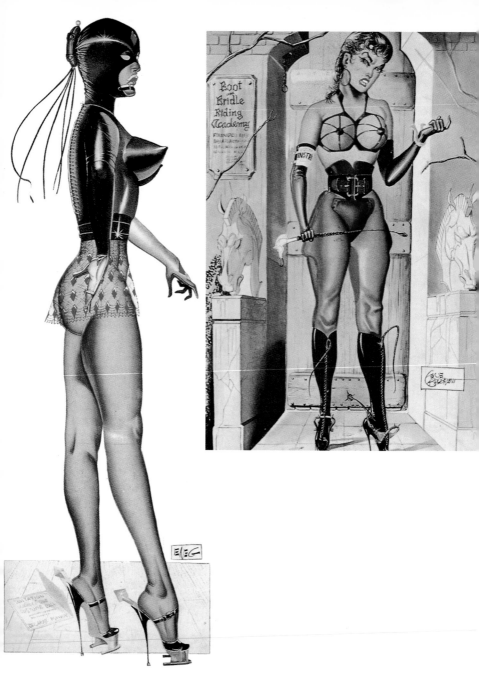

Illustrations for *Exotique*. From left to right: Eneg, Bilbrew, Eneg, Bilbrew. 1958-62

Eric Stanton: Betty Page in *Gwendoline*. 1960

Betty Page as "mistress". Photo Irving Klaw Studio.
1951-56

Jane Birkin in black stockings and gloves, with switch
in hand, in the film by Michel Boisrond, *Catherine et
Cie.* 1969

Until fairly recently, the censors would not allow dogs to appear in soft-porn photos, as this hinted too much at bestiality. The photographer Serge Jacques circumvented this difficulty by photographing "bitches" (left page), before

being able to photograph real dogs (right page). 1980s

Eric Kroll and sadomasochism in *Fetish Girls*, Taschen. 1994

▲ A modern and more user-friendly version of the *chastity belt:* now made of soft, comfortable leather. Photo by Robert Chouraqui. 1990s

▲ The latest fashion in sadomasochistic underwear, a return to
metal, with built-in barbs. Design Kurt Veith (New York).
Photo by Robert Chouraqui. 1997

▲ Patent leather underwear for the
torture chamber. 1970s

Sadomasochistic outfit made of metal and patent leather. Photo by Robert Chouraqui. 1996

The angry mistress and her terrifying underwear. Photo by Lioris. 1996

Christophe Mourthé: The torturer (left) and the willing victim (right). 1997

The chic appeal of leather underwear and the shock value of metal chains. Photos by Christophe Mourthé. 1998

Christophe Mourthé's girls and their elegant sadomasochistic underwear. 1997

Following pages: The height of elegance – sophisticated sadomasochistic
underwear. Photos by Christophe Mourthé. 1998

All the capitals of the world now boast specialist S&M underwear shops which stock the stuff of fantasy.

▲ A shop in Denmark

▶ Velda Lauder models, London. Photos by Robert Chouraqui. 1995

In the closing years of this century, it would seem that innovation in the lingerie industry has been almost entirely restricted to the extreme world of sadomasochism. This is probably a fitting comment on contemporary society and the new woman. Artists, who might just as well be sculptors, give free rein to their imagination and create garments

which are more akin to battle armour and space-suits than lingerie.
◄ Michel Coulon designs. ▲ Valhalla-Coudrer designs. Photos by
Robert Chouraqui. 1996

Designs by Michel Coulon that would not look out of place at the Georges Pompidou Centre in Paris. Photos by Robert Chouraqui. 1996

▲ Women-tables and other pieces of women-furniture
wearing sadomasochistic underwear by Allen Jones. 1971
◄ The indestructible corset makes a comeback. Women's
favourite instrument of torture is now made of vinyl.
Photo Christophe Mourthé. 1998

Lingerie and Eroticism 762 · 763

Copyright · Bildnachweis · Crédits photographiques

Unless otherwise specified, copyright on the works reproduced lies with the respective photographers. Despite intensive research it has not always been possible to establish copyright ownership. Where this is the case we would appreciate notification.

Das Copyright für die abgebildeten Werke liegt, sofern nicht nachfolgend anders aufgeführt, bei den jeweiligen Fotografen und Künstlern. Trotz intensiver Recherche konnten die Urheberrechte nicht in jedem Fall ermittelt werden. Wir bitten ggfs. um Mitteilung an den Verlag.

Sauf mention contraire, le copyright des œuvres reproduites se trouve chez les photographes qui en sont l'auteur. En dépit de toutes nos recherches, il nous a été impossible d'établir les droits d'auteur dans quelques cas. En cas de réclamation, nous vous prions de bien vouloir vous adresser à la maison d'édition.

p. 6: © 1998 Photo: The Estate of Robert Doisneau / Rapho, agence de presse photographique, Paris | pp. 32 center, 33 center and bottom, 43 top, 44, 94 right, 168, 178 top right, 182 top, 183 top, 184 bottom, 185 bottom, 198 left: © 1998 BT Batsford Ltd., London | pp. 48, 73, 74, 75, 76, 77, 80, 87, 89, 120, 122, 123, 124, 125, 138, 139, 140, 141, 143, 144, 161, 163, 164, 165, 169, 180, 181, 182 bottom right and left, 183 bottom right and left, 424 right, 425 right, 426, 427 right, 452, 528, 530, 531, 533, 564/565 and spine: © 1998 Photos: Roger-Viollet, Paris | pp. 59, 109, 110, 111, 564-565, 581 bottom, 582, 586, 587, 588, 589, 715: © 1998 Collection Alexandre Dupouy, dans "Yva Richard – L'âge d'or du fétichisme", Éditions Astarté, Paris | pp. 92/93, 113, 221: © 1998 Photos: Ministère de la Culture – France / AAJHL | p. 129: © 1998 Photo: Horst P. Horst, Richard J. Horst Collection, New York, NY, USA | p. 136, 570: © Man Ray Trust, Paris / VG Bild-Kunst, Bonn 1998 | p. 173: © 1998 Photo: Keystone, Paris | p. 195, 201 right, 232 right, 233 left, 682, 683, 684, 685, 742, 743: © 1998 Photos: Eric Kroll, San Francisco | p. 204: © VG Bild-Kunst, Bonn 1998 | p. 208: © 1998 Photo: Erwin Blumenfeld | pp. 209, 210, 211, 212, 213, 214, 215, 239, 246, 473 top and front cover: © 1998 Photos: Jeanloup Sieff, Paris | pp. 224, 680, 681: © 1998 Photos: Dahmane Benanteur, Paris | pp. 226, 410, 504, 610, 611, 614, 615, 618, 619, 620/621, 622, 623, 626, 627, 629, 630, 631, 632, 633, 634, 635, 636, 664, 665, 666/667, 674, 675, 676/677, 679, 740, 741: © 1998 Photos: Serge Jacques, Paris | pp. 227, 649, 650, 652, 653, 654, 655, 656: © 1998 Photos: Gilles Néret, Paris | pp. 260, 262, 263, 744, 745 left, 746, 756, 757, 758, 759, 760, 761: © 1998 Photos: Robert Chouraqui, Paris | pp. 264, 265, 496, 497, 498, 499, 748, 749, 750, 751, 752, 753, 754, 755, 762: © 1998 Photos: Christophe Mourthé, Paris | p. 266: © 1998 Photo: Alain Benainous / Gamma / Studio X | p. 267: © 1998 Photo: UK-Press / Gamma / Studio X | pp. 268, 289, 305, 334, 336, 337, 338, 339: © Pierluigi Praturlon/Reporters Associati, Rome | pp. 288, 298, 299, 324: © 1998 Photos: Edimedia, Paris | pp. 296, 297, 301, 311, 356 top, 357 top: © Association Française pour la Diffusion du Patrimoine Photographique, Paris | pp. 302, 350, 351: © 1998 Photos: Editions René Chateau, St. Tropez | p. 313: © 1998 Photo: Philippe Halsman /Magnum Photos | pp. 325, 333, 397: © 1998 Photo: Image-France – Raymond Cauchetier, Paris | p. 393: © 1998 Photo: Productions BELA, Neuilly s/Seine | p. 445: © Salvador Dalí, Fundación Gala – Salvador Dalí / VG Bild-Kunst, Bonn 1998 | p. 518 right: © 1998 Photo: Bulloz | pp. 547, 550, 551, 552, 554, 555, 567, 579: © Collection Alexandre Dupouy, dans "Collections privées de Monsieur X", Éditions Astarté, Paris | p. 598 bottom: © VG Bild-Kunst, Bonn 1998 | p. 599: © VG Bild-Kunst, Bonn 1998 | pp. 606 right, 607 left, 609: © 1998 Photos: Bunny Yeager | pp. 640/641, 642, 643, 644, 645, 646, 647: © 1998 Photos: Benedikt Taschen Verlag GmbH, Cologne | p. 659: © 1998 Photo: Xavier-G. N. | pp. 700/701, 702/703, 763: © 1998 Allen C. Jones, London | pp. 702, 733, 738: © 1998 Eric Stanton | pp. 716, 717, 718, 719, 724, 725: © Collection Alexandre Dupouy, Paris.

FRONT COVER: Jeanloup Sieff: *New York*. 1962
SPINE: Raphaël Kirchner: *The Elegant Corset*. Circa 1900
BACK COVER: Photo Schall for the magazine
Pour Lire à Deux. 1936
PAGE 1: *Three Cheers for the Bride*! Drawing by Siné. 1980
PAGES 2–3: Photo for *La Perla*
PAGE 4: Raquel Welch in *Myra Breckinridge*,
a film by Michael Sarne. 1970
PAGE 5: Comic strip lingerie and one of its heroines: *Torchy*. 1947

© 1998 Benedikt Taschen Verlag GmbH
Hohenzollernring 53, D–50672 Köln
© VG Bild-Kunst, Bonn 1998 for: Hans Bellmer, Richard Lindner, Clovis Trouille
© Man Ray Trust, Paris / VG Bild-Kunst, Bonn 1998 for: Man Ray
© Salvador Dalí, Fundación Gala-Salvador Dalí, VG Bild-Kunst,
Bonn 1998 for: Salvador Dalí
See p. 767 for further copyright information
Text and conception: Gilles Néret, Paris
Graphic design: Catinka Keul, Cologne
Cover design: Angelika Taschen, Cologne
English translation: Sue Rose, London

Printed in Germany
ISBN 3–8228–7629–1